For Jason— Go Dawgs!

Merry Christmas 2008

DOOLEY'S PLAY BOOK

Vince Dooley
illustrations by
Steve Penley

Vince Dooley

Hill Street Press
Athens, Georgia USA

A HILL STREET PRESS BOOK

Published in the United States of America by
Hill Street Press LLC
191 East broad Street | Suite 216
Athens, Georgia 30601 USA

www.hillstreetpress.com

Published in partnership with Dodd Rentz and Entourage Productions, Inc.

Hill Street Press books are available for bulk purchase and in customized
editions. Please contact us for more information.

Artwork by Steve Penley appears courtesy of Linstrum & Matre Artworks (Atlanta, Georgia) (LMartworks.com).
Photography by Robert Matre.

Text and cover design by Bonnie Youngman.

Printed in the United States of America.

ISBN 978-1-58818-187-9

10 9 8 7 6 5 4 3 2 1
First printing

TABLE OF CONTENTS

To all the assistant coaches who were an integral part of the journey, especially two of the greatest: my brother, Bill Dooley, and the late Erk Russell.
–Vince Dooley

The publisher apprecitates the partnership of
Robert Archie Rushton in support of this publication.
His participation is in honor of his late parents,
Dr. Archie Sime Rushton and Betty Johnson Rushton,
both loyal University of Georgia alumni and scholarship donors.

FOREWORD

I was thrilled when asked by Coach Dooley to write the foreword for this book. The thought immediately occurred to me that it would be the only way my name would be a part of the book. Having been a solid-mediocre player at best, his invitation afforded me a singular opportunity to join ranks with my heroes from the past.

Coach Dooley's writings and recollections will stir the blood of the entire Bulldog Nation. Don't expect this book to record the conservative approach to the game for which he was so famous. It will literally involve the reader in all the emotion and excitement that is Georgia football at its best.

How can we forget the Theron Saap "Drought Breaker" of 1957? The "Say Hello to Herschel Walker" touchdown run over Tennessee in 1980? Or my favorite, the "run Lindsay run" touchdown reception against Florida that catapulted our team to the National Championship in 1980. All of these great plays and much more are brought to life eloquently and passionately by Coach Dooley in this book.

But for me there is more—when I read this book and notwithstanding all the great moments of athleticism it recalled, I could not help but think that one name stands above all others as the most important person and influence on our rich football tradition—that person is Vince Dooley.

Enjoy!

Billy Payne
Atlanta, May 2008

INTRODUCTION

Early on, those who became aware of my writing a book have asked me one or more of the following questions: What constitutes a memorable play? Who selected the plays: Why did I choose to feature thirty-four plays? I am sure those same questions are on the minds of many readers as they look into my book.

The answer to the last question is easiest. Obviously, I chose to feature thirty-four plays because of the legendary Herschel Walker, knowing that would please Georgia Bulldog fans everywhere. But, it goes far beyond that correlation. Of the thirty-four plays selected, Herschel was responsible for four of them; twice as many as any other player. I know from first-hand experience that Herschel had so many memorable plays that a book could have been written just on his college experience alone. The only other Georgia player that would come close to Herschel, in the sheer number of memorable plays, would be Charley Trippi. However, the passing of time and lack of media coverage then as compared to today lessens the Trippi comparison.

The number thirty-four also provided a very practical benefit. It put a limit on the number of plays and gave me a framework to work with.

If a poll were taken, I'm sure that most of the Bulldog faithful would agree on the top ten or fifteen plays with Buck Belue to Lindsay Scott being the first in everyone's mind. After the top ten, opinions will vary widely.

One criterion I did use was that the play had to result in a victory for the Bulldogs. There have been several sensational plays made by Georgia football players that would have made the list of thirty-four, had the Bulldogs won the game.

I knew early on that I should provide a diagram for each play to help the reader better understand the dynamic on the field. While researching the plays for the book spanning almost eighty years, I was intrigued by the use of Xs and Os in diagramming defensive and offensive players respectively. The use of the O on offense has remainder virtually unchanged over time. But, the X is no longer used on defense, replaced by a gradual shift to designating a player's specific position, such as S/S for strong safety. It was fun preparing these diagrams in a way that reflected these changes over time.

While I reserved the right to have final say on the plays selected for this book, I sought expertise from some of the greatest Georgia football historians. I am very thankful to my longtime friends Dan Magill, Loran Smith, and Claude Felton for their expertise, help with research, and editorial assistance. All have served the University of Georgia Athletic Association in the Sports Information Office and have written many books and articles on our football program. Their combined experience covering and writing about Bulldog football history spans over 140 years. There is no institution in America that can boast of having three such competent and devoted football historians as these men.

I also sought the expert advice outside the confines of the UGA Athletic Association. Who is better qualified than Atlanta Journal-Constitution sports writer, Tony Barnhart? Tony admits he became hooked on Georgia football in 1965 when he was twelve years old. After graduating from Georgia in 1976, Barnhart write sports for several newspapers before landing what he called his dream job. In 1984, he joined the AJC as a beat writer for the Bulldogs. Since that time, he as served as AJC College Sports Editor and has developed a national reputation for being one of the most respected writers and editors in his field.

I also sought the advice of a small group of Bulldog loyalists who exemplify the word "FAN-atic." I wish I could have reached out to more fans. It would have provided some enthusiastic and controversial opinions on their most memorable plays. Perhaps this book will jog their memory and I will be hearing about the ones missed, or decided against. I tried to cover some of these bases with a chapter of additional, memorable plays at the end of the book.

It is appropriate to thank my good friend Billy Payne for writing the foreword. No one represents the heart and tenacity of a Bulldog better than Billy. His success in leading the 1996 Centennial Olympic Games in Atlanta and currently as chairman of the Augusta National Golf Club is a special source of pride to the "Dawg Nation." He came to Georgia to pursue his academic and athletic goals and for the opportunity to play "Between the Hedges," like his father Porter a generation before him.

The two pictures that are special to me, and certainly dear to Billy, are: one taken when he was two years next to his father in a Bulldog uniform, and one taken twenty years later with his dad while Billy is dressed in a Bulldog uniform. This inspiring father-son relationship produced two outstanding citizens, community servants, and great football players. Billy and his dad were both All-SEC players on championship teams twenty years apart (1948 and 1968). I have often said I never coached a better "60-minute football player" than Billy Payne. He not only could have played a variety of positions, but did on offense, defense, and special teams.

Billy is also the classic example of what Alfred Lord Tennyson describes in "Ulysses" when he writes: "I am part of all that I have met." You really do become a part of all you associate with. I have learned from all the many friends, coaches, and athletes I have worked with through the years; but no one more than Billy Payne. He has provided the old coach with great moment, and that special feeling of pride that a father has when a "son" has done his best.

I also want to thank my good friend, and highly respected writer and attorney, Bob Steed. It was a very pleasant surprise when I found out he was a strong promoter and advocate for Steve Penley. His afterword provides the perfect footnote for the book.

Lastly, I want to thank my good friend, the very talented Steve Penley. I am very proud to do this book with him. I never cease to be amazed at his work, and the following of fans and collectors he has developed. His paintings of the plays featured in this book are magnificent and make all those great moments in Bulldog history come to life in a very special way.

I first became acquainted with Penley's work when Barbara and I visited out good friends, Nelson and Pam Bowers, at their home in Sun Valley, Idaho. I saw for the first time Penley's painting of Teddy Roosevelt and the Rough Riders. I has no idea who this Penley fellow was,

but I really liked the painting. Later, in another part of the house, I saw a painting of a race horse entitled "Sea Biscuit" that almost blew me away. I'm a fan of the Sea Biscuit story, and the painting was superb!

I soon met this talented artist and his lovely wife, Carrie. To my surprise, I found that he was a Georgia graduate and Bulldog fan. He and his father-in-law, J. Carl Nash, have visited us in Athens and we have been to Carrollton to visit their family. It has beem a great privilege to work with Steve on this book, and my admiration for him as a friend and artist continues to grow.

As a special treat, Penley painted a picture (shown on the next page) of Richard Von Gammon, the man behind one of the most interesting stories in football history in the state of Georgia. In 1897, while UGA was playing the University of Virginia, fullback Von Gammon was severely injured and later died. There was an outcry across the state, proclaiming football as too brutal. This movement was taken up by the state legislature who passed a bill to outlaw the game in the state. Ultimately, Von Gammon's mother, citing her son's true love for the game, appealed to the Governor to save the game. At her request, he subsequently vetoed the bill, saving the game of football forever in Georgia. However, twenty-four years later, in 1921, Georgia and Virginia played again and UVA presented UGA with a bright medallion (shown in the painting on the next page) of Von Gammon and bearing the inscription: "A mother's love prevails." The medallion hangs today in the Butts-Mehre building on the UGA campus.

I hope all who read this book enjoy it as a special journey through the great history of Georgia football.

GEORGIA BULLDOGS IN THE COLLEGE HALL OF FAME

It usually is the extraordinary players that produce memorable plays. The University of Georgia has eleven All-Americans who have been recognized with college footballs highest honor, the Hall of Fame. There are also three Georgia coaches who have been inducted into the College Football Hall of Fame

Glenn "Pop" Warner (11) was inducted in 1951. He began his coaching career at Georgia compiling a 7-4 record in 1895 and 1896. Warner went on to coach at several other schools recording 319 career victories.

Bob McWhorter (1) was inducted in 1954. He was Georgia's first All-American in 1913. McWhorter was All-Southern four consecutive years, 1910-1913.

Frank Sinkwich (7) was inducted in 1954. He was Georgia's first Heisman Trophy winner (1942) and led UGA to wins in the Orange and Rose Bowls. He earned All-American honors in 1941 and 1942.

Charley Trippi (13) was inducted in 1959. He captained Georgia's undefeated, untied Sugar Bowl team of 1946, and was named All-American that year. Trippi won the Maxwell Award and was also runner-up in the Heisman balloting trophy in 1946. He went on to a great career in the NFL with the Chicago Cardinals where he earned All-Pro honors in 1947. He also led the Cardinals on the 1947 NFL championship team.

Vernon "Catfish" Smith (3) was inducted in 1979. He was the star of the 1929 Georgia-Yale game in which Sanford Stadium was dedicated. Smith scored all fifteen points in that game. The Bulldogs won 15-0. He received All-American honors in 1931.

Bill Hartman (12) was inducted in 1984. He captained the Bulldogs in 1937 when he was named All-SEC and All-American. After playing for the Washington Redskins, Bill served on the Georgia coaching staff with Wally Butts. Later, he became a volunteer kicking coach under Vince Dooley.

Fran Tarkenton (10) was inducted in 1987. He was an All-America quarterback who led Georgia to the SEC championship and an Orange Bowl victory in 1959. He went on to an All-Pro career in the NFL with the Minnesota Vikings and New York Giants and, for years, help all the NFP records.

Vince Dooley (6) was inducted in 1994. He coached the Bulldogs for twenty-five years (1964-88) and led UGA to a consensus national championship in 1980. His 1968 team was recognized as national champions in one poll. His teams posted six SEC titles (1966, '68, '76, '80, '81, and '82), twenty bowl games, and 201 victories. He retired from coaching as Georgia's winningest coach.

Wally Butts (8) was inducted in 1997. He coached the Bulldogs form 1939-1960 leading Georgia to a twenty-two-year record of 140-86-9, six bowl games and four SEC championships, the aational championship in 1942 and again in 1946.

Bill Stanfill (4) was inducted in 1998. He was a consensus All-American and winner of the Outland Trophy in 1968. He went on to an All-Pro career with the Miami Dolphins winning two Super Bowls.

Herschel Walker (9) was inducted in 1999. He was a three-time consensus All-American, 1982 Heisman Trophy winner and led Georgia to three SEC titles (1980-81-82) and the 1980 national championship.

Terry Hoage (5) was inducted in 2000. He was a two-time consensus All-American, Academic All-American (1982-83) and finished fifth in the 1983 Heisman Trophy balloting. He went on to a thirteen-year NFL career.

Kevin Butler (14) was inducted in 2001. He became the first kicker ever inducted into the Hall of Fame. He was an All-American in 1983 and 1984. He is most remembered for his 60-yard field goal with eleven seconds left to beat Clemson, 26-23, in 1984. He went on to a record-setting career with the Chicago Bears including a 1986 Super Bowl Championship.

John Rauch (2) was inducted in 2003. He started every game at quarterback for four years (1945-48) and his 4,044 career passing yards set an NCAA record. Rauch led UGA to two SEC titles (1946 and '48) and was a first team All-American in '48.

Georgia has several players that made All-American and should eventually be inducted into the Hall of Fame. There is one player, however, that without a doubt will automatically be accepted as soon as he becomes eligible and that is David Pollack. Other than Herschel Walker, he is the only other three time consensus All-American in Bulldog history (2002, '03, and '04).

CATFISH SMITH
VERSUS
YALE UNIVERSITY
OCTOBER 12, 1929

"Of all Georgia's past heroes whom
I have met since coming to Athens,
there was no one that I enjoyed
more than Catfish Smith."

Dr. Steadman Vincent Stanford, Georgia's Faculty Chairman of Athletics and President and later Chancellor of the University System of Georgia, talked the administration of Yale into venturing south to play Georgia in its inaugural game in Sanford Stadium. It was the first time that Yale, a perennial power in college football at the time, traveled outside of the Eastern United States to play a football game. Yale, long considered "Georgia's Mother Institution," agreed to come and honor its Southern counterpart since a number of Yale scholars had come south to teach at the University, including the school's first president, Abraham Baldwin. The "Dedication Day" was named in his honor.

The Dedication Day game climaxed the biggest "football weekend" gala Athens had ever experienced with governors, senators, congressmen, generals, institution presidents and other dignitaries attending the game. All 30,000 seats in the new stadium were sold out and for the first time ever. NBC radio was in Athens to broadcast the game nationally.

At the official dedication, the Yale team was lead onto the field by its band, which earlier, had paraded downtown and saluted all of the Georgians watching, with "Hail to Georgia down in Dixie." This warmed up the Athens crowd who were somewhat suspicious of these "Yankees," invading the South again. Nevertheless, mighty Yale was very courteous to its "little sister" school, before the game since they planned to "show off the New England brand of football to the people of Dixie."

After the Yale band and team had taken its place on the field, the Georgia Band then led the Georgia team onto the field to the roar of the crowd. For the first time ever a Georgia team had an opponent "between the hedges," though the famous hedges were just infants at the time.

It was a hot and humid day between the hedges and it was a factor in favor of the Bulldogs. Robert Hall, Yale Blocking Back, whom I met in New York several years ago, said his "team wore long wool stockings and wool uniforms and that the pre-game ceremony lasted what seemed like an hour and the heat and humidity were unbearable. We were finished before the game started." What really finished the Yale team off was a fired up bunch of Georgia Bulldogs led by sophomore Vernon "Catfish" Smith who scored all the points that day in the 15-0 win. The game jump started "Catfish's" career and he later went on to earn All-American Honors and induction into the College Football Hall of Fame.

In the second quarter, Smith recovered a blocked punt in the end zone for a touchdown, added the extra point and shortly thereafter Catfish tackled Yale's star Albie Booth in the end zone for a safety. In the trash talking lingo of these early years of football, Booth got up after being tackled hard, and told Catfish, "that doesn't go around here Smith," and Smith replied, " the only thing that doesn't go around here is you Albie"!

The lightening blow that finished off the Yale team

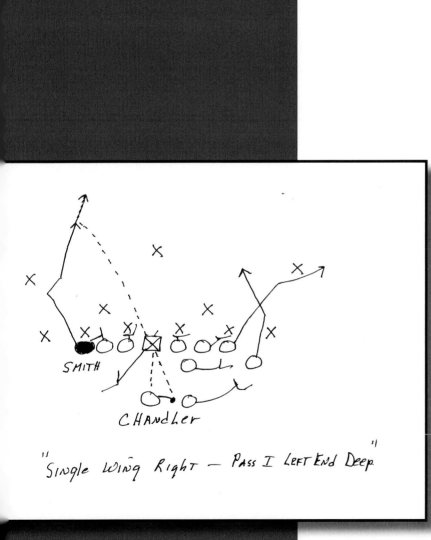

SMITH

CHANDLER

"Single Wing Right — Pass I Left End Deep."

came in the final quarter. Georgia was using the "Notre Dame System" installed by head coach, Harry Mehre which consisted of the single wing formations employed either by shifting into the formation or lining up without the shift. On the play, wing Spurgeon Chandler—who later became one of the greatest pitchers in baseball history for the New York Yankees—lined up at tailback and Catfish Smith at left end. On the direct snap from center, Chandler took a step to the right, followed by a shoulder fake, giving Smith time to release, and make his move before hitting Smith for the touchdown. Smith said, "I faked the halfback to the right and I went to the outside and "Spurge" threw me a perfect pass."

After a brief stint coaching college football, "Catfish" Smith went into the Air Force and retired to Maui, Hawaii. I went to see him in 1969 on an Air Force coach lecture tour and spent a full day with him touring the Island and watching his son pitch baseball in a little league game. Several years later his son came to Athens as a member of the California football team that played Georgia between the hedges on September 11, 1976. Catfish was there as a proud dad, but he was also a very proud Georgia Bulldog, who maintained constant contact with his University, even while living in Hawaii and subsequently California. He was returned to his beloved Georgia for his final resting place. There is a monument to him in the family plot in Bolingbrook, Georgia just north of his home town of Macon where he was born and later starred at Lanier High School.

Of all Georgia's past heroes whom I have met since coming to Athens, there was no one that I enjoyed more than "Catfish." He was charming, colorful and had a flare about him that charmed all the women. My wife, Barbara, for sure loved him and we still talk about him today.

LAMAR "RACEHORSE" DAVIS

VERSUS AUBURN UNIVERSITY
NOVEMBER 1, 1941

This was the forty-second meeting between these two ancient rivals, which represents the oldest rivalry in the Deep South. All games have been important, but none more important for Georgia than 1941. Early in the season, the Bulldogs got off to a rough start when star tailback, Frank Sinkwich, had his jaw broken in the second game against South Carolina. Playing with a face mask to protect his jaw, Sinkwich and the Bulldogs were tied by Ole Miss and were beaten by Alabama. In a hard hitting contest, both Georgia and Auburn consistently moved the football between the twenty yard lines but could not score any points for nearly the entire contest. The Tigers had three legitimate scoring opportunities, but never crossed the Bulldog goal line. With less than a minute remaining, Auburn punted out-of-bounds at Georgia's 35-yard line, keeping the ball away from the speedy Lamar "Racehorse" Davis as they had tactically done all day.

Davis was a :09.7, 100-yard long striding sprinter; thus dubbed "Racehorse." He was a dangerous threat on kick returns and long pass receptions and had scored on a 50-yard touchdown pass to enable Georgia to tie Ole Miss, 14-14. Thus, the Auburn strategy was to always punt out-of-bounds and NOT to "Racehorse."

Had time been kept on the field in those days, Auburn might have considered in hind sight punting away from Davis but not out of bounds for as it turned out there were only three seconds left to play when the ball went out-of-bounds. With three seconds to play there was time for one play. Had the ball stayed in bounds on the punt, the game would have been over, assuming, of course, "Racehorse" did not return it all the way for a touchdown.

Lamar Davis had a vivid memory of the details of the play which I will relate: "At the time we did not know that there was only time for one more play but we all knew the end of the game was near. In the huddle, "Frankie" Sinkwich called for "Pass 2-ends in Front." This play was designed to put pressure on the safety."

"The play called for both ends to run out routes taking the corner backs with them. "This left me running straight down the right side of the field trying to shake the safety," said Davis.

With the middle cleared out, blocking back and team captain Cliff Kimsey was to slip through the middle and "Frankie would hit him with a wide open field." As it turned out Sinkwich was under pressure from the Auburn rush, and he threw the ball where he thought Kimsey would be. Davis said he "saw out of the corner of my eye that Cliff had trouble making it through the line and knew that I was going to be the only one with a chance to catch the ball."

Davis said he remembered "the gun going off" as the ball was in the air. He made the catch and outran at least one defender to the goal line. He said he heard "staggering and muttering" from the defender. One of the sports writers covering the game at the time reported that "three Auburn men were within a yard" of Davis "when he grabbed the cowhide (the ball was made from cow skin in those days instead of pig skin) and went over for the winning score." The play covered sixty-five yards and the Bulldogs won, 7-0.

Davis said that when the game was over "the referee wanted the ball but he never got it back! That ball was mine!" Today the ball sits in the University of Georgia Hall of Fame."

As a side note, Davis said his friend, Leo Costa, kicked the extra point that was unnecessary since the game was over but he said he was glad he did because "he established a record of scoring, at least a point in every game for 3 years.

A case could be made according to Loran Smith in his book, *Between the Hedges*, for Lamar "Racehorse" Davis' 65-yard touchdown reception being the "most dramatic touchdown play" in Georgia history. The rational being the gun went off when Frank Sinkwichs' pass was in the air. I agree, and for sure without the play Georgia would not have gone to its first bowl, the Orange Bowl, where Frank Sinkwich put on one of the greatest performances in bowl history; which leads us into the next most memorable play.

"The Auburn strategy was to always punt out-of-bounds and, no matter what, NOT to Racehorse. It backfired, resulting in arguably the most dramatic touchdown play in Georgia history."

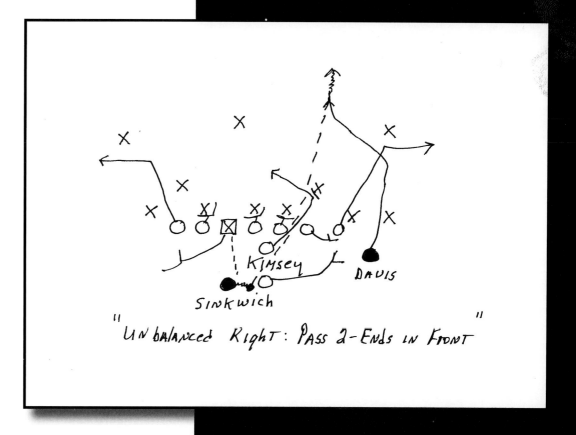

"Unbalanced Right: Pass 2-Ends in Front"

FRANK SINKWICH
VERSUS
TEXAS CHRISTIAN UNIVERSITY
AT THE ORANGE BOWL
JANUARY 1, 1942

All-American Frank Sinkwich, playing with a broken jaw, put on an offensive show still regarded as one of the greatest in any bowl game as the Bulldogs trounced Texas Christian, 40-26, in the 1942 Orange Bowl. This was Georgia's first appearance in a post season game. Sinkwich completed nine of thirteen passes for three touch-

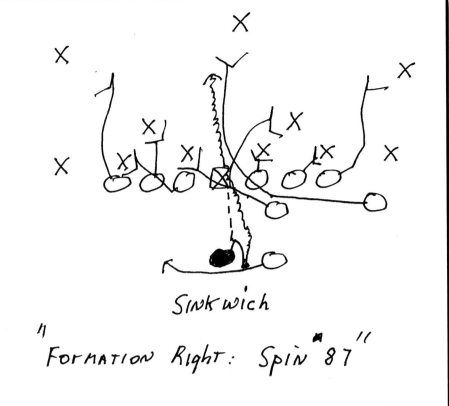

Sinkwich

"Formation Right: Spin "87""

"All-American Frank
Sinkwich, playing with
a broken jaw, put on
an offensive show still
regarded as one of the
greatest in the history of
bowl games."

downs including a 61-yard touchdown pass to Melvin Conger, a 60-yard touchdown pass to Cliff Kimsey and a 15-yard touchdown pass to Lamar "Racehorse" Davis—for a total of 243 yards in the air. On the ground Sinkwich rushed for 139 yards including a 43-yard touchdown run, giving him a grand total of 382 yards, an amazing feat especially in that era of football. This remains an Orange Bowl record.

His 43-yard touchdown run up the middle off the play called "Spin 87" was Sinkwich's favorite play throughout his career. "Spin 87" best utilized his incredible quickness getting to the line of scrimmage. The play exploited his startling speed so effectively that twenty-five of his thirty rushing touchdowns came off of "spin 87."

On the play, Sinkwich lined up in the single wing tailback position. He would take a direct snap from the center, execute a "half-spin" and fake to the fullback and then accelerate straight up the middle behind the trap block of the blocking back and the strong side end who would pull and lead him through the hole.

Sinkwich was an extremely durable back who had stout hips and thighs and a gifted "swivel hip" running technique. Those assets, combined with his explosive power, enabled him to break an enormous number of tackles. When the defense would crowd the line of scrimmage it would open up passing opportunities as it did in the Orange Bowl. Sinkwich was truly "Mr. Inside." When he and Charley Trippi ("Mr. Outside") worked together in the same backfield, they were a dynamo for the defense to reckon with. They were certainly the fore-runners of the famed Army duo Doc Blanchard, "Mr. Inside," and Glen Davis, "Mr. Outside" of the late 1940s.

With Trippi at tailback and Sinkwich at fullback, which only happened occasionally in 1942, that fire-power combination was deadly in the single wing. I can only imagine what those two could do in the modern day "spread offense" which is not much more than a "spread single wing" with option opportunities.

Charley Trippi told me, while I was discussing his famous run against Georgia Tech in 1942, that he would love to have played in the "spread offense" of today. I can only imagine him in today's spread utilizing his incredible running and passing ability. Imagine putting Sinkwich at fullback with Trippi at tailback, which added the inside running threat. Then add to that the option and passing threat – all in the same backfield. This dual threat would have produced an offense that coaches can only dream of today, unless you coached defense against them.

CHARLEY TRIPPI

VERSUS

GEORGIA TECH

NOVEMBER 28, 1942

Despite coming off a devastating loss to Auburn, Georgia was excited that the winner of this game would receive an invitation to Pasadena and the Rose Bowl. Before the upset by Auburn, the Bulldogs were riding high having come back in the fourth quarter against the then Rose Bowl favorite, Alabama, from a 0-10 deficit to win, 21-10. The Associated Press voted Georgia number 1 for the first time in school history and the Bulldogs responded by trouncing Florida, 75-0, in Jacksonville.

The team was looking forward to playing Georgia Tech at the end of the season but they had to play Auburn in Colum-

bus before taking on Tech in the big game. The stage was set for one of the biggest disappointments in Georgia's football history. The Bulldogs were ranked No. 1 in the nation and Auburn had lost to Florida which was beaten by Georgia, 75-0. The Bulldog's were looking past Auburn to Georgia Tech and the Tigers were "chomping at the bits" to avenge the lost to Georgia the previous year.

Auburn literally manhandled Georgia, 27-13, with Tiger running back Monk Gafford having a field day. The Bulldogs were devastated and Athenstown and the campus were plunged into gloom. The depression only lasted for a few days when the Rose Bowl committee announced they would invite the winner of the Georgia-Georgia Tech game. The outcome of the game would also determine the SEC Championship and Georgia had never won a conference title.

Georgia Tech had been elevated to No. 1 in most polls and No. 2 in the AP poll. The Georgia players were mad at themselves for their performance in the Auburn game. The stage was set for the Bulldogs to come out swinging and they jumped on their rivals from the start of the game. Both Frank Sinkwich and Charley Trippi, rotating at tailback scored early touchdowns. Then both started operating in the same backfield. The results was devastating for Tech. Trippi practically blew the game open right before half time with a brilliant 86-yard touchdown run.

The play was called "Harvard 29 Pass". Trippi told me that "Harvard" was just a term designated by Coach Butts that meant the fullback would be the ball handler thus the center would snap it to him. In the play Sinkwich took the snap, executed a half spin and handed the ball to Trippi who ran to his right on a sprint out pass. Trippi said that he "always had the option to run on any pass play when the receivers were covered." As he sprinted right looking for his receivers he decided to run. He got some excellent blocks as he cut back and ran eighty-six yards for the touchdown which many say was well over 120 yards considering sprinting right and cutting back, all the way across the field. When he final-

ly crossed the goal line all alone he went to his knees exhausted. The only other football players more exhausted were the Tech players who pursued him on this long jaunt.

Of all the Georgia players I have come to know through my long association with the Bulldogs, I have come to agree with many others that Charley Trippi was the greatest all-around player in the Bulldog's proud history.

When I was a player at Auburn, I was coached by Shug Jordan, who had come from Georgia and brought all those former Georgia players with him. They all talked about Charley Trippi. They bragged that Trippi was the greatest all around football player; but especially talked about him being a super defensive player at safety. That was my position as a sophomore. After a great game Coach Jordan once compared me to Trippi to the media and his comments made the newspaper. That was very special to me for a long time until I saw Trippi play on film later when I was a coach. What a shock, there was no comparison. It was a nice compliment but Coach Jordan obviously got carried away promoting one of his boys. The reality was I was not close to being in his league. Coach Butts thought Trippi was so good on defense he called him a linebacker from the safety position. Georgia Tech's Bobby Dodd called Trippi the greatest safetyman he had ever saw and also the best all around football player he ever saw.

When I was coaching at Georgia, Harry Gilmer, the Alabama All-American who played against Trippi in college and later coached in the pro's told me that Trippi was the best player he ever saw. He said not only could Trippi have played quarterback, he did it for two years in the pros. The same is true in regard to playing tailback, on defense, running, throwing, punting, and returning kicks. You name it and Trippi actually did it and did it magnificently.

There are so many memorable plays that could be added to the great run against Georgia Tech. Perhaps a good ending to this narrative would be Trippi's punt return in the 1945 Oil Bowl described by Coach Butts as "the greatest punt return he ever saw. He started running to his right, reversed his field deep, ran over two Tulsa men at the 15-yard line, lowered the boom on another, and scored. He got just sixty-eight yards, but he ran at least 168."

I saw the run on film and coach Butts did not overstate the incredible run. The only thing he did leave out was when Trippi finally crossed the goal line, he collapsed in the in zone; it was good the team did not pile on in celebration as they do today. There was no danger of that happening since they all had practically collapsed somewhere on the field before Trippi scored.

"I have come to agree with many others that Charley Trippi was the greatest all around player in the Bulldog's proud history."

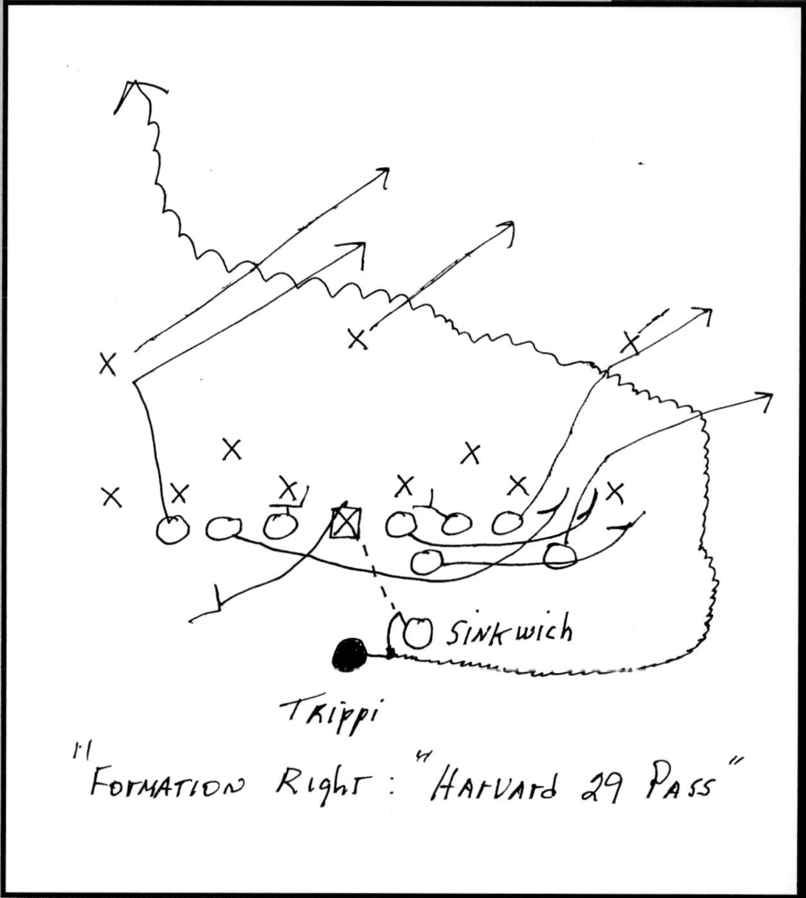

Trippi

"Formation Right: "Harvard 29 Pass""

Sinkwich

THERON
SAPP
VERSUS
GEORGIA
TECH
NOVEMBER 30, 1957

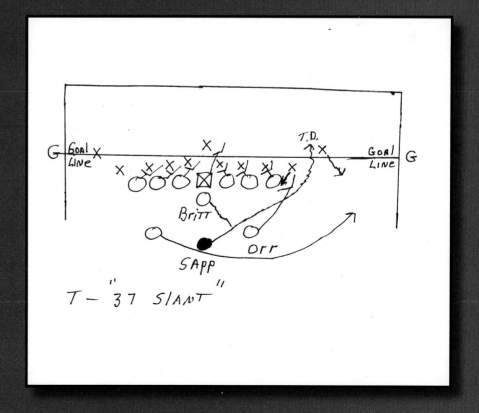

"The 'Drought Breaker's' story is an inspiring one. He survived a neck injury to go on to a brilliant college and pro career."

Long time sports writer and *Georgia Trend* magazine columnist, Gene Asher, said it best, "with a single touchdown Theron Saap did as much for Georgia pride as anyone in Bulldog history." That touchdown was only a one yard run, but "wow" was it ever a huge one under the circumstances.

Georgia had really gone through the hardest of times! Out of the previous five seasons, four were losing seasons, including the 1957 season. Even worse, Georgia Tech, "the ancient enemy," as described by Dan Magill, had beaten the Bulldogs eight straight years. Georgia had not even scored a touchdown against the Yellow Jackets in four years. The "drought," as it was called had kept the disgruntled loyalists in deep depression for almost a decade. On that bitingly cold and windy day in Atlanta in November of 1957, it appeared that the depression of the "Bulldog Faithful" would continue on for another season as the media and the experts had already conceded Tech their ninth victory in a row.

However, everybody underestimated the drive and determination of Theron Sapp, one of the most dedicated Bulldogs ever to wear the Red and Black. That dogged determination became very evident early on when Sapp went against the advice of his doctor and his coach, Wally Butts, not to play at Georgia after he had cracked three vertebrae in his neck in a scrimmage in the state's annual North-South High School All-Star football game.

Saap was determined to play and spent his freshman year at Georgia in a body cast. He spent the next year on the "B" team proving that he was capable of playing despite his injured neck. The next year (1956), he was third string fullback and finally moved up to the starting position in 1957. Then in the final game, against the state rival, he earned the immortal title "as the man who broke the drought."

The "drive" that ended the famine started in the third quarter when Sapp recovered a Tech fumble at midfield. On the scoring drive, Sapp rushed for thirty-five of the fifty yards on "nine bruising carries." Fifty years later, Sapp recalled exactly what happened on the drive that endeared him forever in the hearts of the Bulldog Nation.

"We had driven the ball to the Georgia Tech one yard line," Sapp recalled. "On third down, Charley Britt tried a quarterback sneak but was stopped for no gain. It was fourth down and back in the huddle all of the linemen were saying, 'Give it to Sapp, give it to Sapp … I said, yeah, yeah, give it to me.' We were on a roll and I knew that I could get into the end zone."

Britt called "37-Slant." The play was designed for the quarterback to give the ball to the fullback, off right tackle, with the lineman (Nat Dye and Ray Cooper) blocking down and the right halfback (Jimmy Orr) blocking the end out. That is the way that it's drawn up in the playbook but as with every play, the blocking and route of the ball carrier can change depending on the movement of the defense. That is exactly what happened. As Tech's defensive end slanted down hard inside, Orr blocked the end inside,

the way that he was slanting and "Thundering Theron," ran just outside the end to score the winning touchdown.

Georgia's defense held Tech scoreless in the fourth quarter and the game ended with the score Georgia winning, 7-0. Sapp remembered that "the crowd poured onto the field and the celebration was unbelievable." He remembered that "fan mail came from all over the country." Sapp said that the response was so overwhelming in the state, "that a group of prisoners at Reidsville State Prison had listened to the game on the radio and said that they almost had a riot when we won."

The "Drought Breaker's" story is an inspiring one. He survived the neck injury through hard work, grit and determination. He made All-Southeastern, became captain of his team in 1958, and had his jersey retired. Only three other Georgia heroes—Frank Sinkwich (Heisman), Charley Trippi, (Maxwell) and Herschel Walker, (Heisman)—have had their jerseys retired. After college, Sapp played eight years of pro ball and helped the Philadelphia Eagles to the NFL championship in 1959.

Despite his remarkable career and all of the great memories that go with it, "breaking the drought," stands alone for this Bulldog hero whom I talked to in the spring of 2008. "It was truly an amazing experience that I will never forget, and I was fortunate to be a part of it. It had a huge impact on my life and continues to do so fifty years later."

CHARLEY BRITT

VERSUS

UNIVERSITY OF FLORIDA

NOVEMBER 7, 1959

Before the 1959 season, Georgia was picked to finish ninth in the then ten team conference after finishing last the previous year. However, aided by the return to Georgia of the beloved Defensive Coordinator Coach J.B. "Ears" Whitworth, the Bulldogs upset Alabama, 17-3, in the opening game and began winning conference games with startling regularity. The critical games when I was coaching at Georgia were Florida and Auburn which were always played "back to back." Both games were traditional rivals and both traditionally had good football teams. I have said many times that the toughest challenge our teams faced annually in my twenty-five years at Georgia were to play those two rival teams back to back! If you beat them both you were most always the SEC champion. Before the SEC championship game came to Atlanta in 1994 there was no way to win the SEC championship if you lost to both Auburn and Florida.

"I was scouting for Auburn that day in Jacksonville and I witnessed first-hand Britt's incredible performance. I knew we had our hands full."

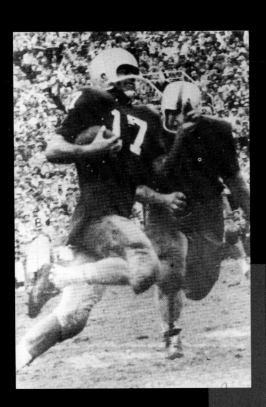

Thus, in 1959, Georgia faced the daunting task of playing those rivals back to back with no history of success against them in previous years. Prior to 1959, Georgia had lost to Florida six times out of seven games and to Auburn six times in a row.

Prior to the Florida game, Coach Wally Butts made a controversial decision to start Charley Britt at Quarterback in that game despite the fact that Fran Tarkenton had been the regular starter that year. Britt, an exceptional athlete, was assigned as the starter at defensive safety. Coach Butts' theory was that Tarkenton had been overworked carrying the load in all of the games up to that point.

Britt responded with a sensational game in which, according to Tarkenton, "He did it all." He led Georgia to two early touchdowns. He passed to Bobby Towns for a 34-yard touchdown, and earlier had engineered a drive that resulted in his calling a halfback pass, Bobby Walden to Gordon Kelley for a touchdown. Switching to defense, Britt made a couple of remarkable plays that involved Florida's Bobby Joe Green, who later punted for the Chicago Bears in the NFL.

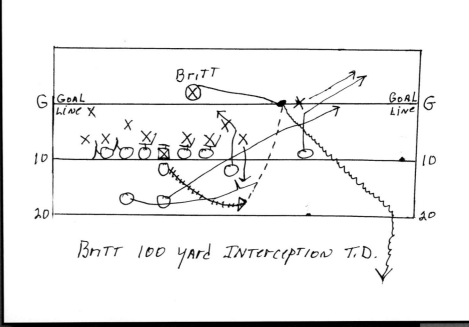

Green was an outstanding kicker, but he also executed a "quick kick" that had been very successful for the Gators. Britt had picked up from the Gator films a "tip" that allowed him to not only neutralize Florida's quick kick but capitalized on the Florida weapon.

The "quick kick" used by Florida was the same one employed by Bobby Dodd at Georgia Tech which had been highly successful for the Yellow Jackets. Ray Graves, Florida's head coach, had been the defensive coordinator under Coach Dodd at Tech and brought it to Florida.

Green executed the quick kick for Florida by lining up at the left half position in a split backfield and receiving a direct snap from the center. He then turned at an angle and kicked the ball sideways over the safety's head. Britt noticed that in order for the center to snap the ball to Green, the quarterback lined up under the center had to move his "left leg back out of necessity in order for the ball to be snapped to Green". Britt said that from his safety position he "could clearly see this, and I would just turn my back to the line of scrimmage and just run! They tried this twice and I caught both kicks in the air and returned them for substantial yardage."

Earlier in the game, this same Bobby Joe Green, who was the SEC sprint champion caught a pass around the Gators 30-yard line and was out in front on the way to a sure 70-yard touchdown. Britt, "running for his life" after seeing Coach Butts' scowling face on the sideline, ran Green down at the two yard line and the Bulldogs defense held, keeping the Gators out of the end zone.

But the most memorable of all the great plays Britt had that day came late in the third quarter with the Gators trailing by twelve points. Florida had marched deep into Georgia territory with a good chance of cutting the deficit and gaining the momentum. It was fourth down and goal at the eight yard line and Florida threw a pass that Britt intercepted and returned 100 yards for a touchdown, finishing off the Gators. Britt recalls that "Pat Dye, to this day, says that he tipped the ball, and it has been a standing joke between us. I always say I was never aware that he tipped the ball!" Britt said that he "remembered catching it just behind the goal line pretty low to the ground and already had a pretty good head of stem up and was able to outrun everybody to the end zone."

After Britt scored and returned to the sidelines, he said that Coach Butts, ever the perfectionist, came up to him and said "you know you took a real chance running that ball out of the end zone ... and by the way, you had the ball under the wrong arm and you did not start putting on speed until you got to the fifty yard line!" At that point Britt said, "Coach Butts, can I ask one question?" "What," Coach Butts responded. "How was it for distance?" Coach Butts looked dumbfounded but later on the "Little Round Man" came up to Britt "and kissed me on the top of my head!" Georgia went on to beat Florida, 21-10, setting the stage for the championship game the next week against Auburn. Tarkenton, who was destined to be the hero in that game, reflected on all Britt had done in the Florida game and said, "Thanks to Britt we won."

I was scouting for Auburn that day in Jacksonville and I witnessed first-hand Britt's incredible performance. After seeing Georgia perform that day, I knew that we (Auburn) would have our hands full the next week in Athens despite the fact that the Tigers were favorites having lost only one game in three years at that time. I was in Athens the following week. We had more than our hands full, as Tarkenton led the team to victory just as Britt had done the previous week against Florida. Those two wins clinched the championship for Georgia.

FRAN TARKENTON TO BILL HERRON

VERSUS

AUBURN UNIVERSITY

NOVEMBER 14, 1959

This game was for the SEC championship. Twelfth-ranked Georgia was seeking its first title in eleven seasons, but the opponent was eighth-ranked Auburn, which had lost only one game since November of 1956. I had returned to Auburn as an assistant coach that year after a stint in the Marine Corps. In 1957, undefeated Auburn won the SEC and National championships and, in 1958, was unbeaten again.

In the 1959 game the Bulldogs were hosting the Tigers in Athens for the first time in thirty years and only the second time in the previous forty-one years. The game, since 1916, had been played in Columbus, Georgia.

Mid-way through the fourth quarter, Auburn blocked a Georgia punt setting up a Tiger go ahead touchdown, 13-7. After stopping Georgia, Auburn had the ball close to mid-field with a good chance to run out the clock and win the game. I was in the press box at the time and we called for our quarterback Bryant Harvard to roll out on a pass

play, but to RUN the ball, and not put it in the air. After faking a pass while sprinting out, the ball was not tucked away. Bill Herron knocked the ball out. It was recovered by future Auburn coach, Pat Dye, at the Auburn 35-yard line. I pounded my fist on the table. I could not believe what had happened and almost jumped out of the press box. Tarkenton moved the team to Auburn's 10-yard line after completing a pass, making it second and one. But the next two plays lost three yards and the Bulldogs were faced with fourth and four at the 13-yard line, on the right hash mark. Tarkenton called time out with less than a minute left on the clock. Then the "Peerless Pilot," as the incomparable Dan Magill often called him, proceeded to design a play with specific instructions to his teammates.

He split his right end to the sidelines and told his left end, Bill Herron, to block, counting "1,001, 1,002, 1,003, and 1,004" and then release for the left corner of the end zone. He told his left half back, Bobby Walden, to "run a hook curl inside to pull the defense to the middle of the field away from Herron." He then turned to Bobby Towns, his right half back and leading receiver on the team, and told him that he was going to decoy him on "a post corner route since Auburn will be expecting me to come to you." He told the rest of the team to block right since he was going to roll that way and throw back to Herron.

The play was executed to perfection though Herron only blocked about half of the prescribed time count (1,001-1,002) before he released. The left half back, Walden, followed Herron in tandem for a few yards until the end broke for the corner. The hook curl by Walden appeared to hold the Auburn corner momentarily, just enough for Herron to pull away from him, catching the ball right at the goal line a few yards from the flag. Tarkenton rolled slightly to the right and ran about seven yards deep before pulling up to throw. That depth helped the play since Au-

burn's back side end came hard off the corner and jumped high in Tarkington's' face, but the "scrambler's" pass was perfect, hitting Herron to the outside.

There were 30 seconds left when Durwood Pennington, known as "the automatic toe," went into the game to kick the extra point to win the game, 14-13. The story has often been told, that Pennington came to the sidelines after the kick, and his teammates were congratulating him on winning the game. He responded quickly, with "oh no we were already ahead." His teammates got a big laugh and still kid him today about him thinking the game was already won and not having the pressure of kicking the winning extra point. The story appears to be apocryphal. For sure, Pennington has long denied it.

In any event the episode was a fitting ending to one of the most memorable and certainly the most unique plays ever in Georgia's football history.

"Tarkenton designed and executed one of the most memorable and certainly the most unique plays ever in Georgia's football history."

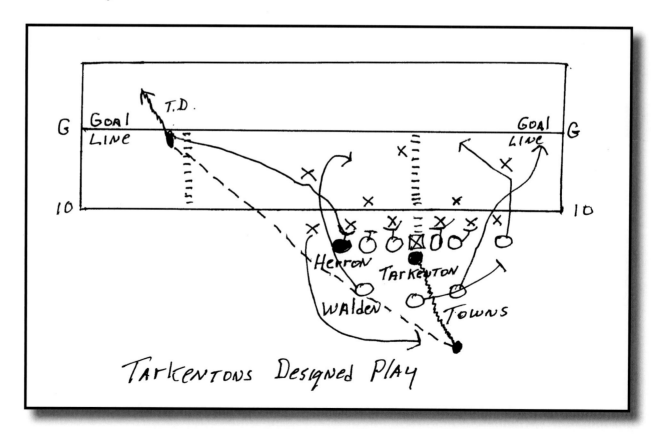

TarKentons Designed Play

BOBBY ETTER

VERSUS UNIVERSITY OF FLORIDA

NOVEMBER 7, 1964

I will never forget my first game as the Bulldog head coach against the Florida Gators in Jacksonville. I was very familiar with that game having scouted Georgia for eight years in Jacksonville while an assistant coach at Auburn. During those eight years at Auburn, I scouted all of our opponents throughout the South, but there was never a game that I enjoyed scouting more than the Georgia-Florida game in Jacksonville. It was like a mid-season bowl game and I enjoyed the festivities. I would go to the "Georgia-Florida Breakfast", and then to the Florida luncheon, enjoying the events while picking up scouting tips. It was a fun way to scout. During that stretch Georgia did not fare well, losing ten out of twelve games. Florida was highly favored in 1964, my first year as head coach. The Gators were ranked ninth in the country and Georgia had not beaten a ranked opponent since 1950. But we had a group of "Battling Bulldogs." Among them was our kicker, Bobby Etter, one of the most unique players that I ever had the privilege of coaching.

Etter was already at Georgia when we arrived. He was signed by Coach Johnny Griffith's staff for several reasons, physical strength not being one of them. When I first saw him I was somewhat startled by this frail little specimen. Soaking wet, he could not have weighed over 155 pounds, but he had been a great athlete in high school, playing basketball and baseball. He was the place kicker and was coached by his dad, Red Etter, who was one of the finest high school coaches in the country. Bobby had a good sense of humor and quipped that his greatest asset might have been his best friend, Dickey Phillips, a highly recruited lineman whom Georgia signed. Etter was convinced the Georgia coaches felt that Phillips would be homesick without his best buddy so they gave Etter a scholarship too. Both enjoyed outstanding great careers at Georgia.

Etter was a typical straight toe kicker, which was the prevalent style at the time. He tied his toe with a string behind his calf muscle to lock his ankle. That was the only thing that was typical about Etter. As a group, kickers march to the tune of a different drummer but Etter set a new standard in that regard. First of all he was a straight-A math major and later earned his doctorate degree at Rice. I often said that since he was so brilliant no one could coach him since no coach could properly communicate with him. So we let him coach himself setting his own routine. Etter was an excellent kicker with his best game coming in 1965 in a 15-7 upset win over mighty Michigan in Ann Arbor. Etter kicked three field goals which essentially was the difference in the game.

But it was Etter's performance, though not as a kicker, in the Florida game in 1964 that was the most memorable. His touchdown run on a bobbled snap to beat the Gators endeared him to the Georgia people and earned for him induction into the Georgia–Florida Game Hall of Fame.

As Etter so correctly put it, "nobody gave us a chance when we went down to Jacksonville to play Florida." As mentioned previously, the Gators, ranked ninth in the country, were heavy favorites and had a history of recent success against the Bulldogs. Georgia was unranked but hungry, disciplined and unified. With a sound defense and a grinding offense we hung in there against Florida and with the scored tied, 7-7, we drove to the five yard-line and then bogged down. The ball was on the left hash mark. I sent Etter in to attempt the short field goal that would put us ahead. But the snap, was low and our holder, Barry Wilson, could not handle the ball. The bobbled ball rolled toward Etter who scooped it up as he and the team immediately went into our "FIRE" situation. Etter said "everything was like a dream, it happened so fast." He said, "Instinct set in because we practiced the 'fire' situation every week." The "Fire" call simply meant that something had gone wrong on the field goal or extra point attempt. Everyone was to shout out and repeat the 'fire' called by the holder and kicker. This told our wing backs to go out for a pass on their side and the tight ends to block down.

Etter picked the ball up running around left end, seeing that Florida's end had rushed hard inside. As he ran to his left he put the ball up attempting to pass, though Etter never remembered doing that. This caused the Florida cornerback to stay back and cover our wingback who was out for a pass in the end zone. Etter then seized the opportunity to run and he got a great block by Wilson which gave him "just enough room to get to the corner of the end zone." As he reached the flag in the corner he executed what he called the "Fosbury Flop," high jumping backwards in the end zone. "The Fosbury Flop" later became in vogue in the high jump when it proved to gain greater height in the event by jumping or flopping over the bar head first and backward. Etter was simply ahead of his time as he performed the "Etter Flop" to score the touchdown and win the game, 14-7. Etter said that "it all felt like a dream, and today over forty years ago it still doesn't seem quite real."

When Etter finished his career at Georgia, he played a year with the Falcons. While he was a very accurate kicker his range was limited due to his frail body and

> "I will never forget my first game as the Bulldog head coach against the Florida Gators in Jacksonville. The winning touchdown was scored by a later college math professor and world class Bridge player doing the 'Fosbury Flop.'"

skinny legs. Realizing this short-coming, his scientific brain "kicked in" and he found a way to get more distance on his kicks. He incorporated a steel rod in his shoe from the toe to the heel that angled up to the top of the shoe. The rod not only permanently locked his ankle, but the added weight increased his kicking range over ten yards and made him a very effective pro kicker. However the added weight in the shoe had its effect on his little body as he would awkwardly limp onto the field for each extra point and field goal. He would have had a long career in the pro's but the NFL didn't take kindly to his innovation and outlawed such structural equipment. The new rule virtually ended Etter's career.

After finishing his PhD in mathematics at Rice University, he became a professor at Sacramento State University where he has been teaching for over twenty years. During his down times from teaching he sharpened his card skills to become a world class bridge player. When school is out you will often find him in Las Vegas competing in world class duplicate Bridge tournaments.

Without a doubt Dr. Bobby Etter, math professor, world class Bridge player, and former pro and college football player, is the most unique athlete that I have ever coached or known in my fifty-two-year career in college athletics. It is fitting that he would be remembered by scoring a winning touchdown as a kicker, against an arch rival, on one of the most unique and memorable plays in Georgia's football history.

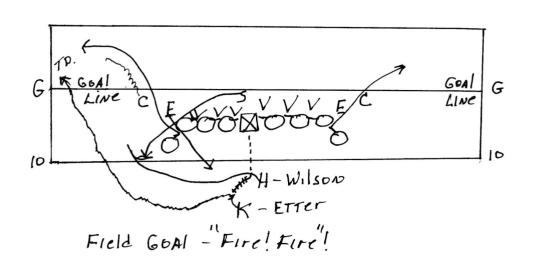

Field Goal - "Fire! Fire!"

GEORGE PATTON

VERSUS

UNIVERSITY OF ALABAMA

SEPTEMBER 18, 1965

Alabama had defeated Georgia five consecutive seasons and was coming off a national championship year in 1964, a two touchdown favorite over the Bulldogs when the teams met in Athens.

This game marked my second season at Georgia. Let's flashback. My first game as a head coach the previous year was against this same Alabama team. I often said

32

that it was a heck of a way for a young coach to start a career; to play a team that would become National Champions, in their backyard in Tuscaloosa, with Bear Bryant their coach and Joe Namath their quarterback. Since I was thirty-one at the time and didn't know better, I thought that we could pull a major upset and win the game. I got a real education as a head coach that night in 1964. There were moments of success at the start in which General George Patton sacked Namath on his first pass attempt.

The excitement was short lived as that was the only time Namath was on the ground that night. To prove it, at the end of the game, I recall, Namath's jersey was immaculate, except for one green spot on his shoulder. "Broadway Joe", as he later became known, completed sixteen of nineteen passes and didn't throw the ball at all in the fourth quarter, thanks to the magnanamity of Coach Bryant as the Tide beat us, 31-3.

General George Patton, nick-named by Dan Magill for the great World War II general, was converted, from quarterback to defensive tackle after he came to Georgia. Patton made his presence known that night in Tuscaloosa in 1964. His sacking Namath was a prelude to making one of the most memorable defensives plays in Georgia's history. Between the hedges in 1965, Alabama held special meaning for George since he was from Alabama (Tuscumbia) and his older brother, Jim, had played for the Crimson Tide. A family feud was brewing!

We got off to a 3-0 lead that next year, but Alabama with Steve Sloan at quarterback, had driven into our territory at the 44-yard line. Sloan then attempted a play action (fake to the fullback) quick pass on a slant to the flanker but cornerback Joe Burson had the receiver covered so Sloan hesitated at the line and Jiggy Smaha, our other tackle, hit him low from the blind side as defensive end, Jerry Varnado put pressure on him with a rush from the strong side. The ball went flying into the air. General George, who was lined up outside of the offensive right tackle, conscious of containing the quarterback inside, held his ground at the line of scrimmage. Then Patton said, "the ball popped up in my hands and I knew what I had to do." Patton with his long stride ran fifty-six yards for the touchdown escorted by Varnado, now an ordained minister in Athens, and Burson, who later coached in high school and college. George said that he was totally exhausted, as Varnado and the entire team piled on him. "I couldn't breathe," Patton remembers. "It was a steaming hot day with the thermometer reading 110 degrees on the field." He said that he had "never run over twenty yards in my life." He had just gone fifty-six and was piled on with no breathing room. To top it all, he was on the kick-off team. We forgot to take him out and rest him so he had to cover the ensuing kick-off!

The General, who was lean anyway, lost almost fifteen pounds that day, but said that the experience was "something for a lifetime." He still enjoys recalling it today. George's dad, who was at the game, called George's big brother, Jim, the ex-Alabama player turned attorney at home and gave him periodic updates. Big brother Jim later quipped that it was bad enough losing to Georgia but having to listen to brother George the rest of his life was almost too much to take. Aside from the family kidding, big brother Jim was mighty proud of his little brother who went on to earn All-American honors in 1966 as he captained the Georgia team to our first SEC championship.

Patton's spectacular interception and touchdown run gave us a 10-0 lead in the 1965 game, but the defending national champions caught us and went ahead, 17-10, later in the fourth quarter, which set the stage for two more memorable back-to-back plays to upset the national champions.

"It was a heck of a way for a young coach to start a career . . . against a national championship team coached by Bear Bryant with Joe Namoth as quarterback. The education payed off for me the next year."

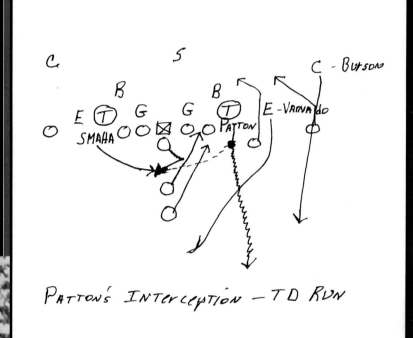

PATTON'S INTERCEPTION — TD RUN

KIRBY MOORE to PAT HODGSON to BOB TAYLOR VERSUS UNIVERSITY OF ALABAMA

SEPTEMBER 18, 1965

Georgia's 10-0 lead highlighted by defensive tackle George Patton's interception and fifty-six-yard touchdown return evaporated in the fourth quarter when Alabama scored with a little over three minutes left to take the lead, 17-10. Not having a "quick strike" offense at the time, we had to rely on a big play: "the Flea-Flicker."

As we concluded fall practice in preparation for our opener with Alabama we had a plan for every situation except one summed up by the following question: What are we going to do if we get behind and we need a quick score, especially considering our offense was not suited to a quick strike passing game? I remembered a play we used to run in the streets of Mobile we called "Pass and Lateral." The passer would throw a high ball to the receiver, who would then jump up and catch it and immediately lateral to a trailing player. We put in a version of the play during our light work day (no pads day). The players, always in good spirits on a "no pads" day, especially at the end of "two-a-day" practices, embraced the play as a light moment in celebrating the end of "two-a-days."

We practiced the play several times but it never worked in our drills. The principles involved were, the quarterback, (Kirby Moore) who would pass to the receiv-

38

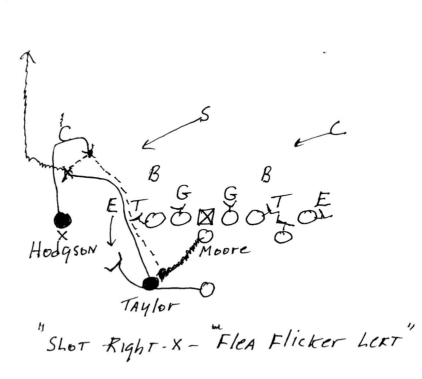

"Slot Right-X — "Flea Flicker Left""

"Not having a 'quick strike offense,' we had to rely on a big play: the Flea-Flicker. We had practiced the play several times but it never worked like it did on this day!"

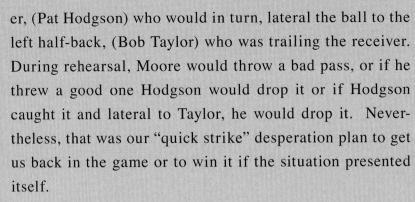

er, (Pat Hodgson) who would in turn, lateral the ball to the left half-back, (Bob Taylor) who was trailing the receiver. During rehearsal, Moore would throw a bad pass, or if he threw a good one Hodgson would drop it or if Hodgson caught it and lateral to Taylor, he would drop it. Nevertheless, that was our "quick strike" desperation plan to get us back in the game or to win it if the situation presented itself.

When Alabama scored and went ahead after we had battled them so hard all day, I knew it was time to run the quick strike "Flea-Flicker". I don't remember why we gave it that name. Now of course the "Flea-Flicker" is called by the pros as a play where the quarterback hands the ball to the tailback who runs to the line and turns and tosses it back to the quarterback who in turn throws a long pass down field. The play that we put in, and which is in most every team's repertoire today, is more appropriately called the "Hook and Lateral."

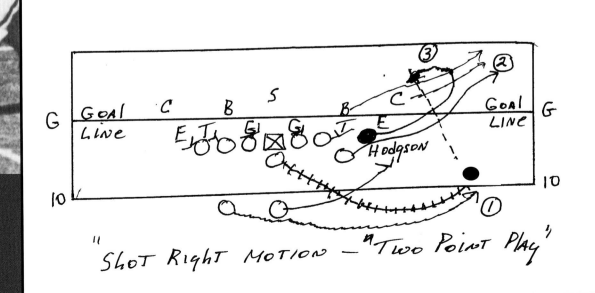

When Georgia returned Alabama's kick after the Tide had scored, Kirby Moore said that someone came into the huddle with my instruction to call the "Flea-Flicker." Moore said, at first he thought that he was kidding and asked him to repeat the call, which he did. Kirby said that he called the play, reminding everyone, that it was the play that we had rehearsed but had never worked. Upon hearing the call, our left-half-back, "Bullet" Bob Taylor, always the serious one, said that he got cold chills: "It scared me to death since I was the one being called upon to produce." Bob took the attitude that the play was going to work because we said so and he believed in his coaches.

Kirby semi-rolled left toward Pat, who was the split-end aligned to the wide side of the field. Kirby threw a low ball to Pat who had to go to his knees to retrieve it. Since he went on his knees, that later became a very controversial issue. But the fact was, Pat never had clear possession as he juggled and then flipped the ball to the trailing Bob Taylor, who then ran seventy-three yards to score. Of interest is that the Alabama safety man at the time was No. 12, later to become legendary Kenny, "Snake" Stabler. Stabler ran up quickly to tackle Hodgson and got lost in the pile.

After we scored, we were still down by one, 17-16. Amid the excitement, one of my coaching role models at the time, the ultra successful Oklahoma coach, Bud Wilkinson, was doing the television color in the game and had come down to the sidelines in anticipation of interviewing the coaches when the game was over. After we scored, Coach Wilkinson, got caught up in the excitement and I turned and saw him and said, "And we're going for two." He excitedly replied, "We've got to!"

When the two point play first became a rule, our plan was to have a play that we called the "two point play," to be used only to win a game late and at no other time. We rehearsed it each week and did so the entire previous year, but we never had an occasion to use it.

After scoring, the team lined up and looked to the sidelines and I gave them the victory sign for the two point play, and they responded without hesitation.

The quarterback had four options on the play, as he rolled out to his right:

1.   To hit the left half-back in motion
2.   Hit the slot-back in the corner of the end zone
3.   Look for the end curling back to the inside
4.   If nobody was open, run the ball

Since we rehearsed the play over a long period of time, we found that as the quarterback rolled past the end on the hook curl route, that the linebackers and defensive backs would forget about him as they pursued the rolling out of the quarterback. Kirby remembered how the play worked so well in practice and told Pat to get open in the end zone, that he would come back to him as he rolled inside. As Pat curled, he remembered Kirby rolling by him and he said, "A huge hole opened up and Kirby hit me right in the numbers."

We went up, 18-17. There was still about two minutes left in the game and Alabama was not finished. They had been national champions the previous year (1964) and after our game, they went through the rest of the schedule undefeated and became national champions again (1965) so this team was not going to be put away easily. Alabama drove down the field and on the last play of the game attempted a tense forty-two yard field goal that was wide which triggered an enormous celebration on the field.

BILL STANFILL
VERSUS
UNIVERSITY OF FLORIDA
NOVEMBER 5, 1966

Both Georgia and Florida were unbeaten in conference play when the two teams locked up for the annual battle in Jacksonville, in 1966. Florida was ranked No. 5 in the nation and Georgia No. 7. The Florida team was regarded as the best ever at the time and were favored by a touchdown over the Bulldogs. The difference in the two teams according to the odd-makers was the Gators' super quarterback and eventual Heisman Trophy winner Steve Spurrier. The expectations were high for Florida, and the Gators were expecting to win their first-ever SEC championship. Only pesky Georgia stood in their way.

To add to the woes of the Bulldogs, sophomore sensation Bill Stanfill had injured his neck in practice on Tuesday before the game and was not expected to play. This was a serious blow to our defense which featured the two best defensive tackles I ever had at Georgia: Stanfill and George Patton. The only two that came close to being compared to them during my twenty-five years of coaching at Georgia were Jimmy Payne and Freddy Gilbert who played for us during the "golden years" of the early 1980s.

Both Stanfill and Patton (like Payne and Gilbert) were tremendous pass rushers. That kind of pressure was needed that day in Jacksonville in order to contain the "Super Gator", a term that defensive coordinator Erk Russell, Stanfill, and the team gave to Spurrier.

Stanfill reminded me that he sprained his neck muscle on Tuesday of the game in the old "bull in the ring" drill. That fundamental drill called "circle butt" was a routine spirited part of practice that the late and beloved Coach Erk Russell conducted with his defensive linemen. It was a freakish type of accident, but the muscle sprain was so bad that Stanfill could not move his neck in either direction. He remained that way the rest of the week and we all thought there was no way he could play in the game.

However, he did play thanks to a lot of time spent in the training room for treatments, including some cortisone to loosen the muscle spasm. More than anything else, game day adrenalin started flowing, Stanfield was magnificent and, typical of great athletes and great competitors, he had a great game harassing the "Super Gator!"

Spurrier, however, was red hot in the first half, as we fell behind, 10-3. Had it not been for Stanfill's play it could have been worse. Late in the opening quarter, Stanfill sacked Spurrier for a six yard loss that kept the Gators out of the end zone. That was the first of several harassments that Stanfill imposed upon the Gator quarterback that day.

Stanfill, along with Patton and Dickey Phillips, put so much pressure on Spurrier that in the second half, off balance and apparently in desperation, Spurrier threw down field just before being sacked. Our safety, Lynn Hughes, intercepted the ball and ran fifty yards for the touchdown that clinched the victory. Georgia outscored Florida, 24-0, in the second half to win, 27-10. Florida had no first downs and gained only thirty-four total yards in the second half while Spurrier was intercepted three times. It was a tremendous second half comeback, typical of the 1966 team. They did the same thing the following week against Auburn, overcoming a 13-0 halftime deficit to win, 13-21, and clinch the SEC championship.

It was a great day for the Bulldogs in Jacksonville in 1966, especially Bill Stanfill who called it "his fondest memory of that year and probably my whole career." It was a nightmare for Florida and the eventual Heisman Trophy winner, Steve Spurrier.

Bill Stanfill went on to become the only Georgia lineman to win the Outland Trophy, symbolic of the best lineman in the country. He was later inducted into the College Hall of Fame in New York and some of his down home remarks that day at the press conference luncheon, are worth noting. Some were particularly relevant to his play in the Florida game against Spurrier.

Stanfill was the last honoree to speak that day in New York following the twelve other inductees. He knew he had to offer something different so he humorously drew on his experience as a country boy growing up on a farm in rural South Georgia.

"Thank you, Hall of Fame for allowing me to join this prestigious fraternity. I too share equally with my fellow inductees and scholar-athletes on what college football meant to them. As a matter of fact, my speech has already been told at least ten times this afternoon and in order not to be redundant, I am just going to shoot from the hip about what college football meant to me.

"I was raised in Cairo, Georgia, a small town in rural southwest Georgia. In the 1950s and 1960s weight-training was not yet the fashionable thing to do. However, I grew up in a weight room and that weight room was the family farm I was raised on. Our family lived off that farm.

"My dad would start off by getting up before light and going to the barn to milk the cow. Well, squeezing on those tits every morning helped me develop tremendous handgrip and strength. That enabled me to head-butt an offensive lineman, grab him under his pads, jerk him off balance and then make a play on the ball.

"I remember summer days walking row after row in the peanut field pulling weeds. Keep in mind the highly mechanized and chemical farming practices we have today were not present back then. Well, some of those weeds were stout and were hard to pull. This chore helped me develop great back and leg strength, which helped me driving off the line of scrimmage, and control the line.

"I remember coming home from football practice late in the afternoon in the fall heading straight to the cotton patch. My job was to pick up the 250-300 pound sheets of cotton the field hands had been picking all day. I would pick up the sheets and hang them on a set of pea scales to get its weight so my daddy would know how much to pay the hands for their day's work. Then I would grab the sheets off of the scales and throw them on the wagon. This chore was much like wrapping up a running back, taking him north while not letting him take me south.

"I remember working my show steer with a halter and show stick, only to have the steer get a bit rambunctious and knock me down in a fresh pile, I might add. Well that taught me to get up, demonstrate to that steer that it was me, not him that still had his manhood intact. Much like in football, you are going to be knocked down but you get right back up and do your best to win the next play and hopefully every play after that.

"I remember my mom telling me that she wanted to fry a couple of chickens for lunch. With that being said, I headed to the ¾ acre chicken pen to catch her two fryers.

It was not an easy task to hem up a chicken in a ¾ acre pen! I actually became pretty good at it over a period of time. I don't know if I was getting quicker or that I loved to eat fried chicken, so you coaches out there, I challenge you to come up with a better agility drill than catching a chicken in a ¾ acre pen.

"I remember certain times of the year dad would tell me we needed to cut pigs today. Well my job was to head up to the hog pen. First, I would get the sows out of the pen. No one wanted to be in the pen with a mad sow when her pigs were squealing. While my dad was setting up the makeshift operating room in the corner of the pen, I would catch a 30-40 pound male pig by the hind legs and pull him back to my dad with and hold its hind legs apart. When that razor hit the pig's skin, you never heard such squealing. When dad finished the surgery, I would mop some oil on the incision and let the pig up where he would run off just a squealing. As I look back at that chore, I really can't say that it helped prepare me for football- but it sure as hell did remind me an awful lot of sacking Steve Spurrier!

"Now I know that you are scratching your head and wondering what I am talking about. This is a football meeting not a 4-H Club gathering. This gets me back to the original point I was asked to make. What did college football mean-to me. So, to Coach Dooley, the University of Georgia and all of college football, from the bottom of my heart, thank you for letting me get off that farm!"

Thank you, Bill, for getting off that farm and coming to Georgia and helping to make me a successful coach. Thanks too for providing the Bulldog Nation with numerous thrills and memories, especially that game in Jacksonville in 1966, against a "Super Gator" named Steve Spurrier.

"It was a great day for the Bulldogs in Jacksonville in 1966, and a nightmare for the eventual Heisman Trophy winner Steve Spurrier."

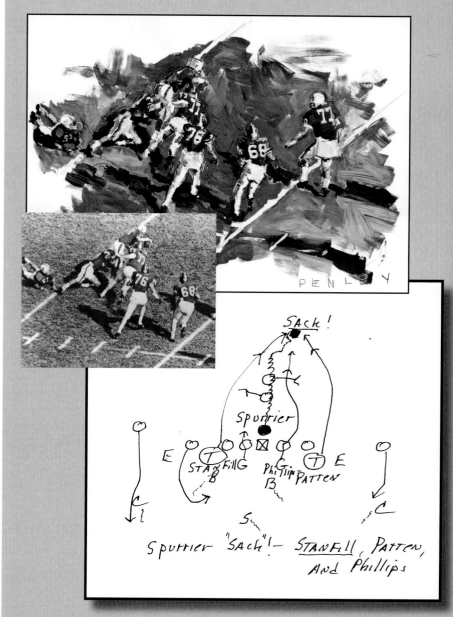

Spurrier "Sack"!- Stanfill, Patten, and Phillips

KENT LAWRENCE

VERSUS
SOUTHERN METHODIST UNIVERSITY

DECEMBER 31, 1966

Most memorable plays in Georgia's football history came either late in the game or late in the third quarter. Very few have come in the first half, and only one came on the second play of the game as it did in the Cotton Bowl in 1966.

It was a cold, windy day in Dallas, Texas, for the 1966 Cotton Bowl. Hayden Fry, the SMU head coach elected to take advantage of the wind after winning the toss and the Mustangs kicked off to us. It was a good coaching decision considering the situation but it turned out to be a bad mistake to give us the ball first.

The head wind had no effect on our tailback, Kent Lawrence, the fastest player that we ever recruited at Georgia. Before he turned his ankle in football, he was recording times in track that would qualify him as a world class sprinter. On the second play of the game from scrimmage, Lawrence found a crack on a routine handoff and sprinted seventy-four yards for a touchdown. The play stunned the Cotton Bowl crowd. Before the first quarter was over our quarterback, Kirby Moore hit our tight end Billy Payne who made a great catch in the end zone and we were up, 17-3. The Bulldogs went on to beat the Southwestern Conference Champion Mustangs, 24-8. Jumping out to an early lead was strange for the 1966 SEC champion Bulldogs because they had to come from behind time after time during the regular season to become champions.

Lawrence, who has served the city of Athens faithfully as a state judge, fondly recalled the explosive play that kept Bulldog fans talking about "Lawrence of Georgia's" incredible speed for years. Lawrence rushed for 149 yards that day breaking the old Georgia bowl record of Frank Sinkwich in the Orange Bowl. His 74-yard scor-

"Most all memorable plays come in the second half of the game. This is the only one in Georgia football history that came on the second play of the game, in the Cotton Bowl in 1966."

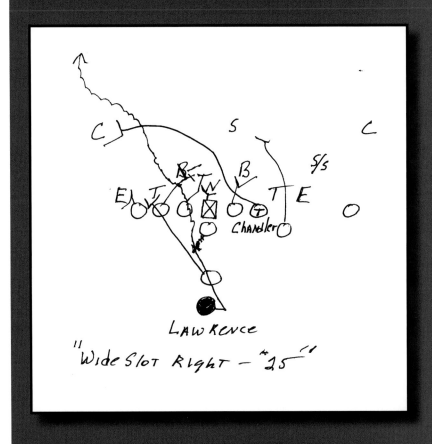

ing play was the longest play in Bulldog bowl history. He was the game's outstanding player, and repeated as most valuable player in The Liberty Bowl the following year.

In addition to Lawrence, Moore was also extremely fast which made us quite effective on offense. SMU was very aware of our outside speed and set their defense wide to counter our strength. From the beginning of the game, SMU's defensive cry was, "Watch 'em Wide." We took advantage of that by concentrating our attack inside. We even adjusted our basic "tailback-off-tackle," which in essence gave us a new play. That play turned out to be Lawrence's touchdown.

On the big play, Moore, after taking the snap, opened left, quickly faked to the fullback and handed the ball to Lawrence who countered with a quick step to the right. It was necessary for Lawrence to counter step since he was so explosive otherwise he would have been running up the rear of our fullback Ronnie Jenkins. Lawrence ran directly behind our left guard, Donald Hayes. Hayes, along with our center Jack Davis, practically annihilated the SMU linebacker and nose guard. Our fullback Jenkins blocked the tackle out and Lawrence was off to the races. Lawrence said, "I was shocked! Just shocked," referring to the size of the hole.

The defensive right corner for SMU might have had a chance to make the tackle but was eliminated by our right tackle Edgar Chandler, the only player agile enough and fast enough to cross the field in front of Lawrence and make the block on the far cornerback. Chandler's block sprung Lawrence, who then cut to the sidelines and outran the rest of the SMU team. After Lawrence crossed the goal line six yards in the end zone he unconsciously did a reverse spike over his head of the ball. While watching the play on tape some forty years later with his son Kelley Lawrence, Kent had forgotten that he had spiked the ball, but his son, who kidded him while they viewed the film, will never let him forget it.

Lawrence did remember Harry "Squab" Jones that legendary character who had been associated with Georgia football since 1910, ran with Kent almost step for step. He picked the ball up in the end zone, brought it to the bench and told Lawrence that he would keep it for him. Squab kept his promise and gave it to Lawrence after the game. As a postscript, Lawrence said that "Squab" always reminded him of saving the Cotton Bowl ball, especially when Kent had tickets to a game that he was not using. "Squab" was known by a generation of Georgia players as a "for profit self-appointed ticket agent," operating during the times that players, under NCAA rules, were allowed to have four tickets for each game. "Squab," for obvious reasons opposed the rule that took the "hard" tickets away from the players, substituting instead, passes for the parents and friends of the players. Lawrence will always be grateful for Squab retrieving the football after his run in the Cotton Bowl. He still has that football today. He will pass it on to his son who will pass it on to subsequent generations in the family as a special treasure.

The greatest last second touchdown drive ever engineered in my coaching career took place on Thanksgiving night in 1971 on Grant Field in Atlanta, Georgia. It was the second of two "day-night" nationally televised games, described by Howard Cosell, who called the two games "the greatest day in college football." The afternoon game was the historic clash between Nebraska and Oklahoma for the national championship dubbed as the "game of the century" with Nebraska victorious, 35-31.

The Georgia–Georgia Tech game that night did not have to take a back seat to the Oklahoma-Nebraska clash when it came to thrills, as the Dogs nipped the Yellow Jackets, 28-24, with Jimmy Poulas going over the top with fourteen seconds to play.

The Georgia drive started on the Bulldogs' 35-yard line with 1:29 on the clock. Tech owned the lead 24-12. Our quarterback, Andy Johnson, went to work running twenty-two yards for a first down at Tech's 43-yard line. Tech's defense stiffened forcing Johnson to throw three

incomplete passes setting up a fourth and ten with fifty-seven seconds left. The fourth down call was both critical and controversial. The best play to call was a pass to our tight end, Mike Greene, but while an excellent blocker and football player, he had the least gifted hands of any of our receivers. But he was a winner and we decided to go with him on a play that we called "88 Pass, Y (tight-end) Delay." Our backs shifted to a slide formation and the back to Greene's side cleared the middle running an "up" route. Meanwhile Green dropped to pass protect and counted "1001-1002-1003" and then released up the middle. Greene got inside the Tech linebacker and Johnson hit him in the hands. Like a champion he made the catch for an 18-yard gain and the critical first down.

Next, Johnson hit our split end Lynn Hunnicutt on two out routes near the sidelines. Lynn went out of bounds to stop the clock each time. After Johnson was thrown for a four-yard loss, he quickly called our last time out with twenty-eight seconds left. We decided to go with "28 Pass Z Out," calling for Johnson to sprint out to the right with maximum protection from the tight end and "I" backs, giving him the option to run or throw. Johnson rolled right, saw our "Z" back flanker Jimmy Shirer, open and hit him in the corner and out of bounds at the one. With 18 seconds to play, without hesitation, we decided to go with our other super sophomore, Jimmy Poulos, to the short side of the field with our classic lead goal line play we called "42." We ran the play out of our wide slot formation, to the wide side of the field. Our offensive lineman fired off quickly preventing penetration by the defense. Our fullback made a good block on one of Tech's linemen, but the other made solid contact with Poulos. However, the "Greek Streak," quick and potent with a deadly surge, barely broke the plane, but it was enough for the touchdown before being driven back. If Poulos had not scored, Tech probably would have won. We had no timeouts, and it is doubtful that we could have cleared the pile and execute a normal sideline pass "clock play." The current clock rule which allows the quarterback to ground the ball quickly was not in the rule books at the time.

When the touchdown was signaled, the Bulldog loyalists in the stands and around the country watching on television went "crazy." Those Sophomore Sensations, Poulos and Johnson also went crazy but the controlled excitement of the quarterback made sure that there was not the slightest chance of Tech winning the game. Johnson said when Poulos scored, "I got so excited that I grabbed Jimmy and embraced him and kept him from throwing the ball in the stands, which he wanted to do. Even though there were only seconds left, I didn't want to give Tech any advantage with a 15-yard penalty!"

It was a thrilling football game and a huge win. We had lost two in a row to Tech, and Auburn had beaten us in the previous game keeping us from going undefeated and winning the SEC Championship. We were excited and as Furman Bisher, sports editor of the *Atlanta Journal-Constitution* wrote: "Georgia hadn't been so happy to win one from Tech since Theron Sapp broke the drought in 1957." Perhaps he was right. The Tech win coupled with a victory in the Gator Bowl game gave us eleven victories, the most in twenty-five years. The win eased the pain of the Auburn loss and the two game losing streaks to Tech.

"The Drive," was the coming out party for the two sensational sophomores Poulos and Johnson who would produce many more memorable plays for the Bulldogs before finishing their great careers.

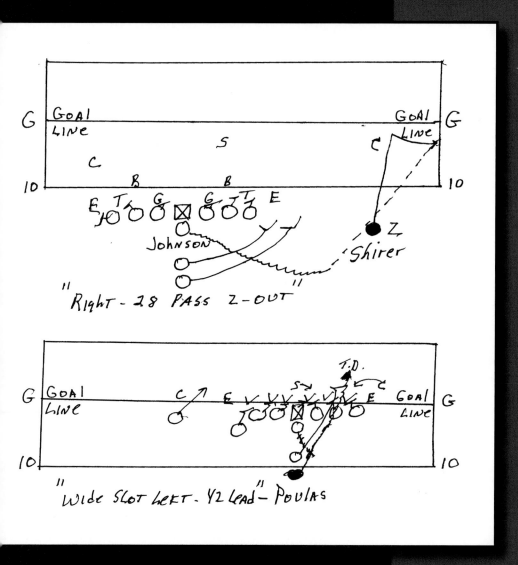

"Right - 28 Pass Z-Out"

"Wide Slot Left - 42 Lead" - Poulas

"The greatest last second touchdown drive ever engineered in my coaching career took place on Thanksgiving night in 1971."

ANDY JOHNSON

VERSUS

UNIVERSITY OF TENNESSEE

NOVEMBER 3, 1973

I have often described the coaching profession as surviving a series of crises. There are no exceptions to this rule. Even the legendary Bear Bryant, the best college football coach of my era, had his crises.

In 1969, Alabama posted a break-even season. Some disgruntled Alabama fans were restless claiming that the Bear was too old and ought to retire. The ultimate embarrassment for Bryant and the Crimson Tide came when the team was beaten by Vanderbilt in Nashville. Bryant was livid and blamed himself for the embarrassment and pledged to do something about it.

Every Sunday afternoon "The Bear Bryant Show" was followed by "The Shug Jordan," each lasting an hour. Some estimated that ninety percent of the people in the state of Alabama tuned in each week to watch the replays of the games. All were seeing the replays for the first time. Everyone was tuned in for the Bryant show after the loss to Vandy, especially the Auburn people who were enjoying every minute of the misfortunes of their arch rival. The Bear, in that deep gravelly voice, said that he was "disgusted with the coaching at Alabama and as the athletic director he was immediately starting a national search for a new coach." This really pleased the Auburn folks who were enjoying the misery of their bitter state rivals. At the end of the season, the entire state again tuned in to the "Bear Bryant Show" with the cameras focused on an upset Bear. He told the audience, again in that unmistaken voice, that as the athletic director "I've

"The game was a thriller if you happened to be a neutral observer. The first four possessions were touchdowns."

searched the country for a football coach but could not find one better than the one we have so I am going to stick with him!" This was vintage Bryant and the Alabama people loved it. He did address the crisis in Tuscaloosa and made changes with his offense. The wishbone would restore Alabama to prominence.

We faced a real crisis on that November 3, 1973 day in Knoxville. We had lost to Vanderbilt and Kentucky back-to-back for the first and only time in my twenty-five years as the Georgia coach. We had a 23-1-1 record against Vanderbilt and a 21-4 record against Kentucky. But if you stick your neck out there year after year, you are going to face such a crisis. Coach Mark Richt, who likely will break all of the coaching records at Georgia, experienced losing to Vandy and Kentucky in 2006. The wolves were howling as his team headed to Auburn to meet a highly favored Tiger team. Coach Richt subsequently enjoyed one of his very best coaching jobs in addressing the crisis by beating Auburn, Georgia Tech and Virginia Tech in the Chick-fil-A Bowl. All were ranked opponents.

We were counted out by everyone in our game against Tennessee in Knoxville that November day in 1973. Tennessee was highly favored on their infamous "Tartan Turf." In anticipation of my losing the game, the Atlanta Journal dispatched to Knoxville a talented young writer, Mike McKenzie, who later rose to writing excellence as the sports editor of the *Kansas City Star*. His assignment was to trail me that day in preparation for a story about my job security.

The game was a spectacular thriller if you happened to be a neutral observer. The first four possessions were touchdowns. We answered each Tennessee touchdown with a touchdown of our own and by half time we had taken the lead, 21-14.

In the third quarter, Tennessee scored seventeen unanswered points and led 31-21 with 10:45 remaining in the fourth quarter. Safety Abb Ansley got things rolling for us with an interception at the Georgia 21-yard line to stop another score by Tennessee. At that point, the Dawgs took control and some say "rose to their finest hour." Andy Johnson took the team on fourteen plays for a touchdown, highlighted by two significant pass plays. The big gainer was a throwback pass from our tailback Horace King to Johnson. Johnson later hit Jimmy Poulos for the touchdown, cutting the lead to 31-28.

The defense stopped Tennessee and with fourth and two at the Tennessee 28-yard line, Coach Bill Battle, in an attempt to regain the momentum, called a fake punt. The Tennessee fullback was thrown for a two yard loss led by Ric Reider who was naturally named "C.C." The Vol partisans were stunned as Georgia drove eighteen yards in four plays to the Tennessee 8-yard line with a little over a minute remaining.

"Power I Left - 45 Lead"

Johnson called for "Power I LF 45 Lead" with the ball going to Glenn Harrison. This was our "bread and butter" goal line play. Johnson admits he "didn't get the ball in the pocket and hit Harrison on the hip!"

The attempted hand-off was so real that the entire right side of Tennessee's defense went after Harrison. Thanks to a "Tartan Turf" bounce, the fumbled ball came right back up into Johnson's hands, and he scored the winning touchdown around the left end.

After the great win over Tennessee, the Bulldogs caught fire and won the next four out of five beating Auburn, Georgia Tech, and Maryland (in the Peach Bowl). The only loss was to Florida who beat us by one point in a game we played well enough to win.

Tennessee's loss to Georgia enabled their head coach Bill Battle to become a multi-millionaire in the business world. Battle was an excellent coach and a real gentleman, but did not survive that crisis and was fired at the end of the season. It turned out to be fortuitous. He started the highly successful company, Collegiate Licensing, which has made him and his family very wealthy. Fortunately, I survived the crisis which gave me an opportunity to coach a few more years before retiring.

The jovial, Ric "C.C." Reider who made the play on the fake punt takes great joy in reminding me that every time that he sees me he "was the one who saved my job" that fateful Saturday afternoon in Knoxville. Thanks "C.C." I will be looking forward to the next reminder!

RAY GOFF
VERSUS
VANDERBILT UNIVERSITY
OCTOBER 18, 1975

For all that Ray Goff accomplished at Georgia he said, "I guess that I will be best remembered for the shoe string play." The "shoe string play" is of course a memorable play, but perhaps it was the in the modern history of Georgia football—even bizarre.

Goff, of course, will be remembered for a lot more than the "shoe string play," and it's appropriate to remind ourselves of his important contributions to Georgia football. In 1975 Goff and Matt Robinson led the "Junkyard Dogs" to the Cotton Bowl. While we didn't win the championship that year I have often said that the 1975 team could "walk with champions" since they beat our three biggest rivals, Florida, Auburn and Georgia Tech all in a row. Up until Coach Mark Richt's team of 2007, all Georgia teams that accomplished that feat were SEC champions like the 1975 team. The 2007 Dawgs "can walk with champions." They, too, defeated our three greatest rivals in a row.

In 1976, due to an early injury to Robinson, Goff became the starting quarterback in the "two quarterback rotation" and never relinquished the starting role. The "one-two punch," utilizing the skillful option running ability of Goff and the excellent passing ability of Robinson, led us to the SEC championship. In the Alabama game for instance, Robinson ran and threw for two touchdowns while Goff directed a touchdown drive, grinding out rushing the ball as he could do so well.

If this book were about great games by individuals instead of memorable plays, Ray Goff's play in the Florida game of that championship year would be right at the top. Down at half time, 27-13, he led a second half rally, scoring twenty-eight unanswered points and beat the Gators, 41-27. Goff threw for two touchdowns and ran for three more. At the conclusion of the year he was named SEC Player of the Year and was voted captain of the SEC championship team. Goff went on to coach the Bulldogs from 1989 to 1995 and compiled a 46-34-1 record, including four bowl invitations and an eighth place national ranking in 1992 following a victory over Ohio State, led by quarterback and current television personality Kirk Herbstreit, in the 1993 Citrus Bowl.

While all Bulldog supporters appreciate Goff's many contributions to the Georgia program Goff said that "it is the 'Shoe-String Play' against Vanderbilt in 1975 that everybody likes to talk about." The main reason was that it was the first of a series of "trick plays" that became associated with the Junkyard Dogs of 1975. Everybody enjoys trick plays, if they work. In Georgia's early football history Coach Alex Cunningham set the bar for using trick plays, taking advantage of a loosely defined rule book. Bulldog historian, the late Dr. John E. Stegman, son of Georgia Coach and Athletic Director Herman J. Stegman, recalls two of the most entertaining "trick plays" in his early history of Georgia football.

In 1910, Georgia went to the Tennessee mountains to play powerful Sewanee, and during the game a thick fog set in so bad that the spectators could see only "vague outlines of the players nearest to them." Coach Cunningham sent in a play "to fit the occasion." On the snap of the ball, the left halfback, George Woodruff, threw his helmet down field. While the Sewanee players gave chase to what they "perceived as a pass," Woodruff slipped the ball to the quarterback Hafford Hay who scored a touchdown, undetected by the Sewanee team.

A few years later in 1912, playing Alabama in Columbus, Georgia, Cunningham pulled off the most notorious sleeper play in Bulldog history setting off a riot between the spectators, the coaches, the administrators and the teams. Coach Cunningham had quarterback Alonzo Awtrey, dress in street clothes and carry a water bucket like a manager, on the sidelines. When the ball was snapped, Awtrey dropped his bucket and started running down the field. The left halfback, Tim Bowden, threw him a pass that Awtrey "caught at the 50-yard line and

"While all Bulldog supporters appreciate Goff's many contributions to the Georgia program Goff said that 'it is the 'Shoe String' play against Vanderbilt in 1975 that everbody likes to talk about.'"

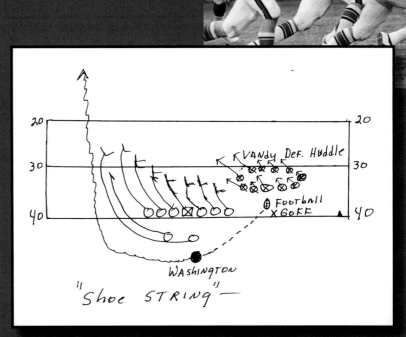

"Shoe STRING"

raced thirty-five yards before being overtaken by a wild-eyed Alabama defender." A thirty minute brawl broke out before the field was cleared and play resumed.

I'm sure there have been other trick plays used at Georgia but none as bizarre as the "Shoe String" play of 1975. I remember the offensive coaches led by our line coach, Jimmy Vickers, coming to me suggesting we to put in the 'shoe string' play against Vanderbilt. Coach Vickers told me that they had used the play at North Carolina when he coached for my brother Bill. The play was designed to take advantage of a defensive team who turned their backs to the line of scrimmage in their defensive huddle. When they diagrammed the play for me I thought it was ridiculous and was against it initially, but reluctantly put the play in our game plan. They talked me into it by emphasizing how it could help us defeat a tough Vandy team in Nashville.

The play was set up by our quarterback (Goff) running a sweep to the sidelines, but staying in bounds. The linemen would partially block and nonchalantly walk to the standing position at the previous spot while the referee returned the ball and put it on the hash mark. The Vanderbilt defense, as they always did, huddled and held hands as their captain called the defense. Meanwhile our flanker speedster, Gene Washington, casually lined up behind the offensive line in the middle of the field, several yards from the hash and the Vandy huddle. Goff then casually walked up to the ball, kneeling down to fake 'tying his shoe.' While in the act of pretending to tie his shoe, Goff said "one of the Vandy players asked him what he was doing." Goff, who almost started laughing, said, "nothing." Then, he shoveled the ball to Washington who ran untouched in the end zone with an avalanche of blockers leading the way. The play stunned the crowd, the Vandy team, and would have stunned the officials, but we tipped them off so that they would confirm the legality of the play. Before the shoestring play we were in a tight game and the play, no doubt, made the game an easy one for us. We won easily, 47-3.

There is a biblical reference: "if you live by the sword you die by the sword." This came about in the Cotton Bowl against Arkansas. At the end of the season we tried a variation of the shoe string knowing Arkansas would be ready for the play. We called the variation "Counter Shoe String." By then we had pulled the end around pass to beat Florida so we were confident that we would have continued success with trick plays.

The "Counter Shoe String" called for Goff to flip the ball to Washington like the "Shoe String," but Washington was going to hand it back to Richard Appleby who would run right and throw a pass to Goff who was an eligible receiver. It looked unstoppable on paper and in practice, but the ball was fumbled and an alert Arkansas defense pounced on the pigskin and that gave them a momentum boost right before half that helped them win the game. I thought to myself at the time, "I never should have approved that damn shoe string play in the first place!"

Those kinds of situations always open the door to light hearted remarks. My Athens friend and humorist Bill Simpson once told the Touchdown Club in Athens that "I was coming through the Little Rock, Arkansas airport, and bent over to tie my shoes and six Arkansas people jumped on me." I cracked up laughing and the whole club had a great laugh. It was such a good story that I used it on several occasions and it always brought a good laugh.

The most memorable trick play of the 1975 season was the end around pass. In the next chapter we'll recall a great moment in Jacksonville and stir the memories of a dramatic play that brought us one of the greatest upset victories in my career at Georgia.

RICHARD APPLEBY TO GENE WASHINGTON

VERSUS UNIVERSITY OF FLORIDA

NOVEMBER 8, 1975

"I just rose to the occasion..."

G oing into the 1975 season, things were not good. "Whatch you got Loran," Smith said: "A Dark Cloud Hung over Georgia football." We had addressed the offensive woes of 1973. The 1974 offense was a high scoring machine operating out of our newly installed veer formation.

The defense however gave up as many points as we were scoring. We had gotten away from our traditional '8 man even front.' We installed instead a seven-man odd front, and the results were a disaster. Our beloved defensive coordinator, Erk Russell would be the first to admit that our defense in 1974 was the worst in the seventeen years that he coached defense in Athens. We were at the bottom of the league in every statistical category. Erk was disappointed and humiliated more than anyone else. The ultimate insult came when an *Atlanta Journal Constitution* headline read, after the season that it would require "a three digit scoreboard" at Georgia to record the opposition's points in 1975!

Erk cut that clipping out and posted it next to his desk where he saw it every day for the next several months. From that time on, he became totally resolved to address the crisis and solve the problem.

The road back to excellence started with the decision to return "8-man front" historically familiar to our coaches. Their experience in that alignment enabled them to make sound decisions and to adjust immediately to any offensive situations. It was a big part of the reason that we became such an effective second half team. The strategy of going back to our base defense was complemented by

"This defensive effort by the Junkyard Dogs was one of the greates that I have ever seen, especially considering how out-manned we were against one of the best-ever Florida teams."

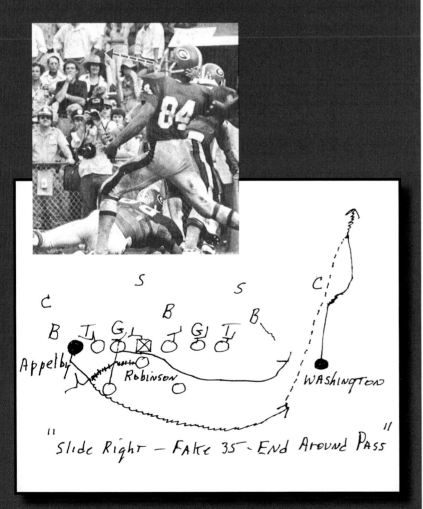

"Slide Right – Fake 35 – End Around Pass"

a highly motivated bunch of defensive fanatics. This turn around in the morale of our defense, more than anything, was attributed to the label "Junkyard Dogs" that became a rallying point of pride. The Junkyard Dog label fit the personnel to a "T."

Since we were such a small but quick and mean team, our good and loyal friend, Jimmy Matthews, husband of Albany Bulldog Club president, Dee, suggested to Erk during the summer months, that we ought to call them "Junkyard Dogs." Erk liked the idea, ran it by me and I was ready to call them anything that would boost our efficiency!

The turnaround in 1975 was furthered aided by UGA president Fred Davison, honoring my request to extend my contract that had one year left. I thought it was appropriate to do so in light of the successes that we had enjoyed by winning two SEC championships. Fortunately, he agreed. The extension put the clamps on any speculation about the immediate future of the program.

After two early losses, this new breed of "Junkyard Dogs" started winning with regularity. The fans responded, especially when James Brown recorded a catchy song written by Happy Howard called "Dooley's Junkyard Dogs." Brown would sing and dance at the games and the fans would go wild rocking and swaying. This created a tremendous atmosphere "between the hedges." The biggest challenges however ahead was outside of our friendly confines of Sanford Stadium. Two of our next three opponents, the so called "The Big Three" (Florida, Auburn and Tech), were on the road. The toughest of these were the Gators in Jacksonville.

Florida had one of its greatest teams ever and was looking once again to winning that elusive first SEC championship. Their offense was truly awesome, averaging 433.5 yards a game, the third best in the nation.

Their rushing offense was awesome, averaging 335.4 yards a game.

Florida scored early taking a 7-0 lead. It stayed that way until right before the half when Alan Leavitt kicked a field goal to make the score 7-3. The Gators marched up and down the field the entire second half as our defense was being stretched to the limit. I was quoted as saying that our Junkyard Dog defense, "clawed, scratched and fought and fell back, but refused to die." Finally with 3:24 left on the clock, Florida leading 7-3, the decision was made to go with our secret weapon: "the end around pass." We had run the end around in earlier games prior to Florida and ran it twice in the Florida game with great success. Our tight end, Richard Appelby, was a great athlete, and could throw it long. We felt confident that it would work if called at the right time. Bill Pace, our offensive coordinator wanted to run it now. With 3:24 left, my first thought was that we were going to leave too much time on the clock for our defense to hold the Florida offense, but I realized that we had to seize the moment. The ball was in the middle of the field, on our 20-yard line, in excellent position for the play.

Matt Robinson was in the game at quarterback and the call was "Fake 35-End Around Pass," flanker right (Gene Washington), slide formation. Glenn Harrison was the dive back, and Robinson made a great fake to him. Appelby, meanwhile, took a step forward and came back around taking the hand off from Robinson with our left guard pulling to lead the way. Washington released quickly down field, "stutter stepped" to block causing the corner back to take the bait, coming up for the run. Then, Washington released to the outside away from the safety. Appelby, meanwhile, stopped, planted his feet and with those long legs and long arms and with a motion described as a "Javelin Thrower", threw the ball over fifty yards in the air. Washington, in the words of Larry Munson, "thinking of Montreal and the Olympics just ran out of his shoes" for the touchdown. The play covered eighty yards. The Georgia fans went absolutely bananas! The noise was deafening and long. Munson went crazy and thinking the old stadium might collapse said, "the girders are bending now."

With all of the excitement, I knew that the game was far from over. I knew that our defense that had been battling all day against this explosive Gator offense had to go back out and somehow stop Florida. It didn't take Florida but a few seconds to respond with 3:05 minutes left. They completed a 46-yard pass and in no time they were on our 35-yard line. On the next play our defensive end, Lawrence Craft hit the Gator quarterback and he coughed up the ball. It was recovered by David Schwak. We held the ball for a little over a minute but had to punt. Florida got it back with 1:42 minutes to play. They drove it 45 yards from their own 34-yard line to our 21-yard line. With seconds remaining, they attempted a field goal to tie the score. The attempt was blocked and the celebration started again.

That defensive effort by the Junkyard Dogs was one of the greatest that I have ever seen, especially considering how out-manned they were. They had stopped the Gators six times inside of our 40-yard line, and reduced their rushing game by 100 yards. The greatest stop of the day was fourth down and one at our 18 yard line that set up the end around pass. But it was the Appelby to Washington pass that brought about one of the greatest upsets in Bulldog history. After the game, Appelby was swarmed by the media. In one of the most memorable statements by a player after one of the most memorable plays of all time, Appelby modestly explained his heroic feat by saying: "I guess you could say that I just rose to the occasion!"

BUCK BELUE TO AMP ARNOLD VERSUS GEORGIA TECH

OCTOBER 15, 1978

From "Under Dogs" to Wonder Dogs" was an apt description of the 1978 Georgia team. During the course of the season, Georgia upset highly favored Clemson, LSU, and Florida. Except for a tie with Auburn, Georgia could have won the SEC Championship. They did win the state championship, coming from behind, after being down 20-0 to beat arch rival Georgia Tech, 29-28.

The star of that "Wonder Dog" team was running back Willie McClendon, who was switched from defensive linebacker to tailback in our newly installed "I" formation. McClendon was a natural as "I" back and had seven 100-plus-yard games that season. Against VMI he broke the thirty-seven year rushing record held by Frank Sinkwich, by totaling 1,312 yards.

At the end of the season, McClendon was elected captain by his teammates receiving the largest majority of votes for a captain ever recorded in my twenty-five years as the Georgia coach. He became the first black player so honored.

The 1978 "Wonder Dogs" were a come- back team all year. They overcame a 16-0 deficit against Kentucky to win, 17-16. They were down at half time against LSU, 17-7, before rallying to win, 24-17, in Baton Rouge. They had to come from behind six times that year, but against Georgia Tech, the "Wonder Dogs" faced their greatest come-back challenge of the year after falling behind, 20-0, midway of the second quarter. It was obvious that we needed a spark and a change of pace at the time. We got it from our freshman quarterback, Buck Belue.

Although only a freshman, Buck had taken a lot of snaps in his young career. He had started for four years at the perennial power house Valdosta High School. That experience helped him to lead the team to one of the greatest come-back victories in Bulldog history. Without a doubt it was the most exciting spectator game ever played "Between the Hedges." That game produced fireworks by both teams! There was a long punt returned for a touchdown, an even longer kick-off return for a touchdown, a surprise successful onside kick, a fourth down touchdown, a game winning two point play, and a last second game winning interception. The lead switched hands four different times before the Bulldog's finally prevailed, 29-28.

Georgia had clawed back after being down, 20-0, to finally gain the lead, 21-20, on Scott Woerner's 72-yard punt return. The celebration lasted only a minute before Georgia Tech's Drew Hill returned the ensuing kick-off 100-plus yards for a touchdown. A successful two point play gave Tech a 28-21 lead.

With 5:42 minutes left, Belue led the team eighty-four yards making two huge fourth down plays on the drive. Backed up in our own territory, the first one came on fourth and two at our own 20-yard line. Buck ran an option, keeping for a first down. We moved it out to the 36-yard line and with fourth and three we decided to go for it again to the astonishment of everybody in the stadium, knowing my habits. I had long been known as a conservative, percentage coach and everyone. Even my wife, Barbara, was flabbergasted that we were going against the odds, not once but twice.

We were on our own 37-yard line with a little over two minutes to play. We had to go for it. The play was "Flanker Right 602 Solid Protection." The "600 series" was a sprint out right, the "2" meant the flanker back running a quick six yard out and the solid protection called for the tight end to stay in and block. It was a one man pass route designed to hit our flanker Amp Arnold on a quick out for the first down.

When Arnold made his out cut he said the "Tech corner back jumped me in man defense and held me. We were both watching Buck and when Buck turned up field, indicating run, the corner back let me go and I turned up field all alone, waving at Buck." Arnold reacted to a rule taught by his coach Charley Whittemore: "If the quarterback is running to you, run away from him!" Buck meanwhile had sprinted out looking to throw the quick out to Amp. "When I saw that Amp was covered, I was looking to run," Buck said. "As I started to run, the corner back

came up in run support and left Amp all alone. By then I knew that I was not going to get the first down running, so I just flipped it down field to Amp." Both Tech's corner back and defensive end, which were fighting off the block of our tight end, almost had Buck in their grasp when he released the ball. Amp caught it and raced forty-two yards for the touchdown. We were behind, 28-27, and there was no question that we were going for two. The first attempt was a semi-roll right throwback pass by Buck looking to hit our right tight end, Mark Hodge, on a 'drag route' parallel to the line. There was pass interference called on the play as three flags came flying out.

The ball was now placed on the 1½-yard line and we called "Power I Right (Formation) 49" which was an option play with the quarterback faking to the tailback before executing the option to either keep the ball or lateral to the trail back. But in the excitement of such critical moments anything can and in this case, did go wrong. The fullback, Jimmy Womack, instead of going left to block, went right! The tailback, Matt Simon, started left for the fake but when he saw Womack go right he went right too.

Buck then turns to fake to Simon. To his surprise Simon had gone the other way and leaving Buck "naked with the football." It might have been a blessing in disguise, because Tech's defensive end had slashed down hard off the corner and Buck reacting, instinctively, as he was falling to his knees was able to get the pitch out to Amp who went in to score untouched. Buck's instinctive reaction to the situation is a great example of why recruiting is the life blood of coaching. The score put Georgia on top, 29-28!

It was only natural that this greatest of all spectator game between Georgia and Georgia Tech was not over yet. With still two minutes left, Tech came storming back down field with their quarterback, Mike Kelly, completing pass after pass. Tech's offense was exceptional with Kelly at quarterback and All-American Eddie Lee Ivery at tailback. Ivery, however, had gotten hurt early in the fourth quarter and was not in the game on that last drive.

Kelly took the Tech team inside our 30-yard line, where a field goal could have won the game, but they were naturally going for the touchdown. We sent in David Archer, a freshman quarterback whom we had worked as a defensive back as part of our "nickel package," our 5 defensive backs scheme used in obvious passing situations. His responsibility was to play man on Tech's tight end. I believe that this was the only play that Archer ever played for Georgia, but he earned his scholarship by intercepting the ball to save the game. As a postscript, Archer transferred to West Georgia College in Carrollton the next year and quarterbacked them to the Division II national championship. But this one play contribution to Georgia football will go down in history as the play that "saved" the Bulldogs' victory over arch rival Georgia Tech in the greatest spectator game to take place "Between The Hedges."

Georgia's freshman hero that day, Buck Belue, would led the Bulldogs to two SEC championships and a national championship, by coming off the bench to lead the Bulldogs to that memorable comeback victory. It will remain one of his greatest thrills. Recalling that moment years later, Buck said, "That was my first thrill wearing the Red and Black between the hedges, and I get chills thinking about it now."

"Georgia freshman hero this day, Buck Belue, would lead the Bulldogs to two SEC championships and a national championship."

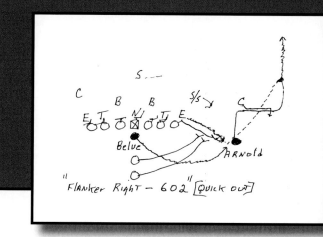

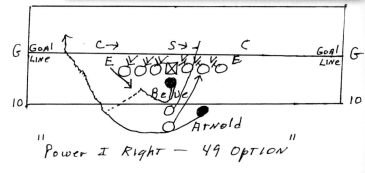

HERSCHEL WALKER VERSUS UNIVERSITY OF TENNESSEE

SEPTEMBER 6, 1980

There was more anticipation heading into the 1980 season than at any time in my coaching career. This was for one reason: a young freshman named Herschel Walker who was recognized as the No. 1 recruit in the country and he was coming to Georgia to start his college career. The hype by the media and the Georgia fans was off the charts. I had a lot of reservations about that much pressure on a freshman. I knew that Herschel was going to be a great player but the question in my mind was just how soon?

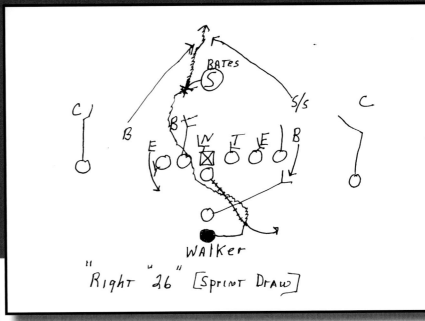

"Right "26" [Sprint Draw]

In high school, Herschel had played in the lowest classification in the state, and I was concerned that the hype and the anticipation might be too much pressure on him. I tried my best to temper the media hype prior to our opener against Tennessee. I did not want to start him but I had a plan to give him an opportunity to play and win the job if he was up to it both physically and mentally.

Donnie McMickens, a fifth year senior deserved to start and Carnie Norris a junior was the back up with Herschel running third at the start of the game. The plan was to give each back two series apiece and evaluate the situation after that. McMickens and Norris both did fine in their rotations, but when Herschel got his chance in the second quarter, it was obvious to everyone that there was a big difference. I remember saying at the time, that when Herschel got the ball I wasn't sure he knew where he was suppose to go but wherever he was going it was somewhere in a hurry!

He won the job on the field and deserved to start the second half. Tennessee was leading 15-3 late in the third quarter. We drove to Tennessee's 16-yard line when Herschel exploded into immortality. The play was "Right (Formation) 26." The "20 Series" was the "draw" series calling for the lineman to delay block, momentarily, then lock up with the defender and take him the way the de-

fender wanted to go. The fullback blocks the end out and the tailback, Herschel, would step to the right and square up to the line as the quarterback, Buck Belue gave the ball to him deep and then fakes a pass.

Any draw play was perfect for Herschel. It gave him time to see what was happening up front. When he saw the hole develop, he utilized his explosive speed to take advantage of it. He told me that was why he loved the "draw" plays which were his favorite.

On his first draw, Herschel got the ball on the 16-yard line. He saw the hole open to the back side and he busted immediately in the secondary. It was at this point that he ran over Tennessee's safety, Bill Bates, to score a touchdown on a play that has been shown around the country a thousand times over.

Herschel said: "I was real nervous when I got the ball. Then I saw this huge hole. When I turned up field I saw Bill and I was going to run by him but he squatted and got low with his head down. I was going so fast that I didn't have time to cut, so I just ran over him."

After he ran over Bates, two defenders hit him from each side at the goal line. Herschel "split" them. Those that saw his run that night went wild and will never forget the moment. Those listening to Larry Munson went wild as he said "We hand it off to Herschel . . . there was a hole . . . five, ten, twelve! Oh you Herschel Walker! My God Almighty! He ran right through two men! Herschel Walker ran over two men. They had him dead inside the nine . . . Herschel Walker went sixteen yards. He drove right over orange shirts, driving with those big thighs. My God . . . a freshman!"

Herschel scored again early in the fourth quarter from the nine to make it 15-15. Rex Robinson kicked the extra point to put Georgia ahead, 16-15. As is often the case, the game was far from over. In the last two minutes, Tennessee drove to our five yard line needing only a field goal to win. They went for the touchdown pitching the ball to their tailback on a sweep. Our walk-on linebacker, Nate Taylor, hit the Tennessee back behind the line sticking his head gear into the ball causing it to pop out. Pat McShea recovered on the one yard line.

We could not move it out for a first down. We sent Jim Broadway—a walk-on who started the game because our regular kicker Mark Malkiewicz missed the game with an injury—into the game in a desperate situation. Broadway, earlier in the game, sliced a kick so I was about as uptight as I had ever been on the sidelines. Broadway kicking deep from the end zone, responded by punting the ball forty-seven yards which put Tennessee out of field goal range. Our defense held for a victory which set the stage for our march to the national championship.

Herschel Walker became the talk of the town, and his No. 34 was later retired and will live forever in Bulldog history. Herschel will always be in the forefront of Bulldog memories, and it all began this fateful night in Knoxville. It is an interesting post script that Herschel wore No. 43 in high school.

It is normal in the recruiting process to accommodate recruits, especially highly regarded ones with their favorite number. The exception we had to that rule was if a senior starter had that number, we would not take it away from him. Keith Middleton was a senior starting linebacker and No. 43. The coaches worried about turning Herschel down for his number, but I was not going to bend on that rule for anyone. Herschel's reaction to our policy immediately defined what type of person, beyond just being a gifted athlete, we had signed. Herschel did not disappoint. He totally understood. From that point on, he demonstrated time and time again that the team came first.

His backfield coach, Mike Cavan, suggested No. 34 a reverse of No. 43. Herschel took it and made it famous. Herschel did not know it at the time, but Chris McCarthy a sophomore and No. 3 fullback had No. 34 and Chris willingly switched to No. 46 when he was told that Herschel would be wearing his old number. McCarthy, who had great respect for Herschel, unselfishly blocked for him for three years. When Herschel won the Heisman in his junior year, he was able to invite two of his teammates to the Heisman festivities in New York. He chose his close friend, defensive back Darryl Jones, and his blocking back, Chris McCarthy. I believe that was part of the reason for choosing Chris came from his appreciation for Chris' exceptional blocking and the other reason being that Chris had willingly given up his No. 34 which Herschel did not know about until after he enrolled at Georgia. It was Herschel's sensitive way of saying "thanks." This gesture is just another insight into Herschel the man and why he remains the most popular football player in Georgia's football history.

SCOTT WOERNER
VERSUS
CLEMSON UNIVERSITY
SEPTEMBER 20, 1980

While Herschel Walker was at the forefront of the success of the 1980 national championship team, he will be the first to tell you that he had a terrific supporting cast. No better example of that fact was cornerback and punt returner, Scott Woerner.

Scott, a high school quarterback, was a superb athlete with an unselfish and exemplary attitude, "Put me wherever you want. I just want to play." We first moved him to halfback before we finally decided to line him up in the defensive secondary. It was a perfect fit! He was also a fearless, reckless punt returner which earned him the nickname authored by Dan McGill, "Woerner the Returner." Scott led the nation in 1980 with an average of 15.7 yards per return, still a Georgia record. He was a consensus All-American and played several years of pro ball. In my opinion, he will become a member of the College Football Hall of Fame. He certainly deserved it.

After the upset win over Tennessee in Knoxville, we manhandled Texas A&M in Athens, 42-0. The Clemson game was next. The Tigers were reaching their stride as a national power. Their 1980 team was led by Homer Jordan, an Athens native who played quarterback at Cedar Shoals High School. The following year, in 1981, he led Clemson to the National Championship.

The first three games in 1980 were the most humid that I can recall in my coaching career. It was almost unbearable in Knoxville and the humidity for the Clemson game was ninety-eight percent! The Clemson team came

to play and knocked us around all day moving up and down the field almost at will. They led us in practically every statistical category except in the kicking game. They had twenty-six first downs to our ten. They had almost twice as many yards, 351 to our 157. They had an incredible ninety plays to our forty-three; controlling the clock for forty minutes to our twenty.

Only in the kicking game and in turnover ratio were we superior. Those stats often win football games. The turnover ratio refers to the number of times that a team turns the ball over compared to the other team. We were a "plus two." Clemson had three of their passes intercepted plus one fumble lost, while we had two fumbles lost. If there ever was an example of an individual winning a game almost by himself, it was Scott Woerner. Against Clemson that day, he accounted for the only two Georgia touchdowns in the 20-16 win and both of them came in the first quarter on long plays. Woerner, who was the game captain that day, was especially psyched for the game which was evident from his body language and enthusiasm following the coin toss.

Clemson was stopped on the first series, and had to punt. Woerner fielded the ball at the 33-yard line. We called for a "middle return," which best suited Woerner's running style. He was fast though he was not a speedster, whom you would try to set up for a side line return. He was not a finesse runner either but he was a tough slashing type runner who could break tackles which made him ideally suited for the middle return. We stayed with that return all year!

With the middle return we always employed three defensive backs about ten yards in front of Scott as personal protectors. The middle protector would take the first man down and the other two would form a wide wedge to let Woerner pick the hole. On the play, Woerner fielded the ball close to the Clemson sideline and with his reckless, slashing style, he got past the first wave of defenders. He only had to shake one man, the kicker, which is normally not a problem. Woerner cut back across the field and the kicker was helpless, as Scott scored in the far corner. He proceeded, on his knee, to "roll seven" with the ball. I had to visit with him about that later.

There were still 13:28 minutes left in the first quarter, and we were up, 7-0. After we kicked off, Clemson came roaring down the field running fourteen plays before missing a field goal. We took over, and went three and out. Clemson, once again, came roaring down the field-- this time driving it all the way to our eleven yard line. It was third down and eleven. Clemson sent a man in motion shadowed by our safety, Jeff Hipp. The motion man ran a post route inside of Jeff, moving into position for a possible touchdown until Woerner, once again, entered the picture.

Scott remembered exactly what happened. "I had the tight end and he blocked, which released me to watch the quarterback and read his moves. Jordan, Clemson's quarterback, rolled to his left. As he squared his shoulders to throw, I was in great position since he didn't see me." Woerner made a classic interception taking the ball at its highest point in the end zone. "When I made the interception, I was running with all that I had and thanks to a block from my old roommate, Chris Welton, I went 98 yards before choking down and getting caught by the Clemson speedster, Chuck McSwain!"

Woerner, a fiery competitor remembered, "Seeing the frustrated expression on the Clemson players and coach's faces as I ran by their bench. Most of them had their mouths agape." Scott enjoyed that. Buck Belue sneaked over the goal line two plays later and we were up 14-0 having run only six plays with no first downs!

Thank goodness for the fourteen points. Clemson continued to push us around the rest of the game. With the score 20-16, in our favor, they drove to our ten yard line with a little over three minutes left on the clock. Our defense had been on the field all day and was exhausted. Clemson called for a pass. The ball ricocheted off of our captain, Frank Ros's head gear and safety Jeff Hipp made the interception at the one. We ran out the clock.

Thanks to Woerner and a team that hung tough and refused to fold under the Clemson pressure, we survived. Woerner's roommate Chris Welton said it best: "Good teams that find a way to win wind up being great teams." The Clemson game was a good lesson for a team that grew in confidence believing that "somehow someway" they could win them all and they did!

"Herschel Walker will be the first to tell you that he had a terrific supporting cast: no better example of that was cornerback Scott Woerner."

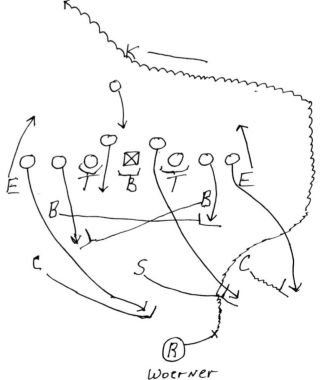

Woerner

Woerner — Middle Punt Return — T.D.

HERSCEL WALKER VERSUS UNIVERSITY OF SOUTH CAROLINA

NOVEMBER 1, 1980

South Carolina has a long history of playing Georgia tough. Overall we have dominated the series so it has been more of a rivalry game for South Carolina than it has been for Georgia. To add to the challenge is the fact that it is always an early game and South Carolina really prepares for us in the off-season. Even when we had great teams, many of the games would go down to the wire. For instance, when we won the SEC championship in 1968, we had to rally from a 0-20 deficit to win late in the game, 21-20.

On some occasions South Carolina would have an excellent team and dealt the Bulldogs a disappointing loss. The only game that Georgia lost in the 1959 championship season was to South Carolina who won convincingly,

"It was the first time the whole country got to see Herschel's amazing speed. They were astounded. Three players had angles on him, but they could not cut him off."

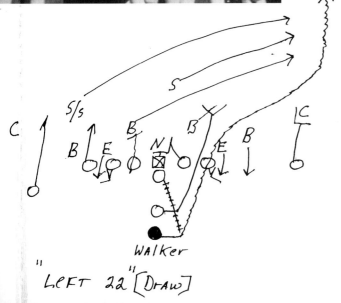

"LEFT 22"[DrAw]

30-14. In 1978, the only regular season loss that we had was to the Gamecocks, led by a sophomore named George Rogers who was instrumental in soundly defeating us 27-10. After the game, Rogers who was from Duluth, made a point to look me up to shake my hand, and I graciously congratulated him. We had lost George in a recruiting battle to South Carolina and I thought that he took particular delight in paying his respects after the victory. The next year Rogers led South Carolina to another win over us and again, George looked me up with that big smile. Again, I congratulated him, but I have to admit that that was getting old! The next year was Rogers' senior year. He and the Gamecocks were looking forward to the first ever three-in-a-row streak over the Dawgs. But this time we had a different breed of Bulldogs and we had a fellow named Herschel Walker. Thanks to the 1980 national champions and Herschel, I never saw George Rogers after another game, though I was tempted to look him up and "pay my respects."

The 1980 game with South Carolina, between the hedges, was a classic preceded by a tremendous buildup. We were 7-0 and ranked fourth in the nation. South Carolina was 6-1 and ranked fourteenth and moving up after a big win over Michigan. The game was nationally televised and media from around the country had poured into Athens to see the match-up between George Rogers, the mid season choice to win the Heisman, and the freshman sensation, Herschel Walker who was making a lot of noise as a Heisman candidate himself.

At the time of the game, Rogers had already rushed for over 1,000 yards averaging 6.4 yards per carry. Walker, who was used sparingly in the Ole Miss game while recovering from an ankle injury, still had numbers similar to Rogers'. He had 877 yards with a 6.2 average per carry. Rogers had ten touchdowns to Walker's nine.

We played exceptionally well in the first half, but only led 3-0, thanks to a fifty-seven yard field goal by Rex Robinson. Rex however had missed an earlier chip shot after a good drive to the South Carolina 22-yard line. Right before the half, we drove to South Carolina's one and instead of sending Herschel over the top on fourth down, we got fancy, attempting to pass which was blocked. South Carolina took over on the one to end the first half.

We took the second half kick off and on third and six, Herschel went seventy-six yards on the "play that was seen around the world." It was the first time that the whole country got to see Herschel and his amazing speed—they were astounded. Three players had angles on him but they couldn't cut him off. Next to the play Buck Belue to Lindsey Scott in the Florida game that year, it is perhaps the most replayed play in Georgia's football history.

"Left 22 Draw" with the flanker back to the wide side and the split end to the short side. The play was our standard "lead draw," indicating the fullback leading the tailback through the hole. The "20 Series" was the draw series and the "2" was the number of the hole over the right guard. Our quarterback Buck Belue gives the ball deep to Herschel who stutter steps and reads the block of the linemen who take the defenders where they want to go. Because of the quick start and speed of Herschel we accelerated the blocking some during the course of the season. This adjustment caused the play to, perhaps, become our most productive. As Herschel said, "I love that play. I had the speed to take it the distance."

On the play the right tackle, Tim Morrison, blocked out on their tackle who came up field, expecting a pass. A huge hole opened up. Herschel was in the secondary in a flash behind our fullback Jimmy Wommack who blocked the left defensive linebacker who had drifted deep, expecting a pass. Herschel cut to his right, got a good block from Lindsay Scott on their cornerback. Herschel said, "I hit the sidelines and got in a foot race and kept focused for the goal line." Did he ever! There were three South Carolina backs all with varying angles that could have made the play against most backs but not Herschel. He turned on the after burners and scored, putting us ahead, 10-0.

We increased the lead with another Rex Robinson field goal to make the score 13-0. South Carolina battled back with a field goal and a touchdown to make it 13-10 and they were driving mid way in the fourth quarter. Rogers looked unstoppable. He ran for nine, eight and then seven. South Carolina was on our 16-yard line. Our defense was about out of gas, but so was Rogers. With a "one more time" effort, Scott Woerner penetrated on a corner blitz and Dale Carver hit Rogers who coughed up the ball. Timmy "Seemore" Parks recovered at the sixteen. Coach Erk Russell gave Parks the name "Seemore" because of his big eyes which seemed to roll around. Was I ever glad to see those big eyes rolling around after he recovered the ball!

With Herschel leading the way, we ran the clock down five minutes, finally giving the ball up to South Carolina at the 1-yard-line with forty-five seconds left. A desperation pass was intercepted by Jeff Hipp and the game was over. The entire football world knew about Herschel Walker.

Herschel gained 219 yards on forty-three amazing carries and had that incredible 76-yard run. Rogers gained 168 yards on thirty-five carries and had the fumble on the key drive. Rogers went on to win the Heisman that year and as a senior, perhaps deserved it. He didn't however "out Heisman" Herschel that day. I am grateful George wasn't looking me up to shake my hand!

BUCK BELUE TO LINDSAY SCOTT VERSUS UNIVERSITY OF FLORIDA

NOVEMBER 8, 1980

The greatest and most memorable play in Georgia's illustrious football history, I maintain, was the Buck Belue to Lindsay Scott touchdown pass in the Florida game in 1980. I believe that opinion is shared by the greatest majority of the Bulldog Nation. Not only did that play win the Florida game when hope was all but gone, but it was the catalyst that enabled us to win the national championship that year.

Coming off of our tough win over South Carolina, I knew we had an extraordinary challenge the next week playing our big rival, Florida. Florida at 6-1 was talented and led by freshman quarterback Wayne Peace. In my experience, the toughest challenge we had during my twenty-five years of coaching was playing our two big rivals, Florida and Auburn, back to back. In 1980, because of a schedule adjustment, we had to play South Carolina, Florida, Auburn and Georgia Tech all in a row. It would take some extraordinary good fortune to survive that "murderer's row."

We entered the Florida game 7-0 and ranked number two in the country. We got off to a great start with Herschel Walker going seventy-two yards on a sweep behind excellent blocking. I don't believe a Florida player laid a hand on him. Herschel, who always stood a little taller against the Gators, had a terrific day as he always did in Jacksonville. He gained 235 yards on thirty-seven carries, but his effort was overshadowed by the dramatic comeback play of Belue to Scott.

Florida had an excellent offensive game-plan under coordinator Mike Shanahan who later became famous as the head coach of the Denver Broncos. They spread the field on us lining up with four wide receivers. Our defense was caught off guard, since Florida had not previously used the formation. We had a hard time adjusting to some very talented Florida wide-outs. Chris Collinsworth, later an All-Pro receiver and NFL TV analyst, caught a pass for a touchdown in the second quarter. We were still ahead, 20-10, in the fourth quarter but the momentum changed. Florida's six foot six wide-out, Tyrone Young, who caught ten passes for the day, made the big play for the Gators that switched the momentum. He caught a short pass, we missed a couple of tackles and he went fifty-four yards to our 11-yard line. On the next play Florida scored, went for two and made it 20-18 early in the fourth quarter.

Our offense completely shut down, while Florida continued to move the ball and then kicked a field goal to go up, 21-20, midway into the fourth quarter. Our offense continued to be ineffective, and Florida kicked the ball dead to our eight yard line with 1:35 left to play.

While there were some fans that were eternally optimistic, many left the stadium thinking it was all over. The Gators for sure were "licking their chops." I remember their defensive cornerback celebrating by doing the "funky chicken" at our sidelines. Things certainly didn't look good, especially after Buck lost a yard on the first play and threw an incomplete pass on the second play. Now we were third and eleven on our seven yard line.

Florida's celebration, I thought, was premature. All we needed was a first down to get out of the hole. Coach George Haffner, our Offensive Coordinator, made the right call to get the first down. We were on the right hash mark and the play was "Left (Formation) 76." It was the right call against a deep prevent defense with a three man rush. Buck and I were thinking the same thing at the time. Get the first down, move down the field and let Rex Robinson win it for us with a field goal. We needed eleven yards for the first down. Buck said, "I knew that I had to go to Lindsay to get the first down since he was running a 15-yard square route." Tight end Norris Brown was running a crossing route underneath which was not deep enough for the first down.

After making his fake to Herschel, Buck looked immediately to the left for Lindsay but "he was covered by the linebacker who was in the throwing lane." At that time Buck had pressure on the back side by Florida's defensive end. Nat Hudson had a great block that enabled Buck to scramble right. The linebacker followed Buck, opening the throwing lane. Buck motioned Lindsay over with his hands as he was scrambling, then hit him. I remember saying, "We got it!" referring to the first down.

Lindsay leaped high to catch the pass and as soon as he hit the ground he started running. I thought, "We've got more than a first down." He raced by our sidelines and I started running with him. I felt I was running stride for stride with him for ten yards and then he left me, as 'Lilting Larry Munson' was shouting, "Run Lindsay run."

Initially Lindsay was thinking first down like the rest of us. As he turned to run, after catching the ball, he said: "I saw the strong safety that had an angle, slipped slightly. "I thought that I could get us in field goal range," Lindsay said, "but after I ran a few more yards, I thought, 'Hell, I can take this thing to the house!'" He certainly did, thanks in part to the flanker, Chuck Jones, whose route and partial screen delayed the pursuit of both the corner and the safety during the run.

I remember, after receiving the film the next day, that at least five different Florida players, had they reacted immediately after the catch, could have made the tackle. The reason they didn't, I concluded, was due to their premature celebration which prevented them from being totally focused. It was a great lesson that I referred to often in coaching.

When Lindsay scored with 1:04 left on the clock, we also celebrated too soon and got a 15-yard penalty that gave Florida a chance to make something happen. Suddenly our lead could have been compromised with a premature celebration of our own. Mike Fisher, a Jacksonville "walk-on" who earned a scholarship ended Florida's hopes with an interception. The 26-21 win moved us to No. 1 in the nation, a ranking that we had to hold and defend three more times before the end of the season. "The Play," became the biggest in college football in 1980 and today remains the greatest and most memorable in Georgia's proud history. Buck's pass and Lindsay's run will be replayed and discussed for generations to come.

"'The Play' became the biggest in college football in 1980 and today remains the greatest and most memorable in Georgia's proud history."

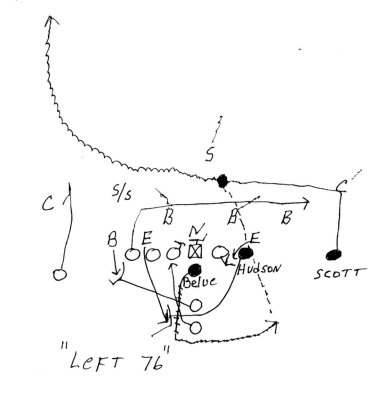

HERSCHEL WALKER

VERSUS GEORGIA TECH

NOVEMBER 29, 1980

"Herschel broke the all-time freshman rushing record set by Tony Dorsett, and he did it in front of the last group of the infamous 'track people,' those die-hards who watched the game from the railroad tracks across the street at the east end of the stadium."

Going into the Georgia Tech game we were 10-0 and ranked No. 1 in the country. Georgia Tech's record was 1-8-1. The Jackets, truthfully, were not very good. We were heavy favorites, but anything can happen in a rival game. Being a historian of sorts, I reminded the team of the 1927 team who went into the Tech game 9-0, ranked No. 1 in two polls, and poised for the Rose Bowl invitation and the national championship. Tech upset Georgia 12-0.

Our team was ready for a battle, however. They had come too far to let this opportunity slip away. As it turned out we won, 31-21, and the game became memorable for two reasons. Herschel broke the all-time freshman rushing record set by Tony Dorsett, and he did it in front of the last group of the infamous "track people," those die-hards who watched the game from the railroad tracks across the street at the east end of the stadium. We started construction immediately after this game to close in the east end zone, adding approximately 21,000 more seats to the stadium.

The track brigade had taken great pride in being a spirited group of supporters for the team. We used to transport the team to the stadium by bus, getting off behind the east end zone. The track people were always there in good spirits to cheer the team. Prior to the Alabama game in 1976, they came early. There were 10,000 jammed onto the trestle by Friday night at 7:00 p.m. After spending the night, they naturally were in great spirits for the game. The players loved the track people, and all have great memories of those wild fans on game day.

The track people were especially fired up for the Tech game. They wanted their last game on the tracks to be the game that Herschel Walker broke the NCAA rushing record. Tech, on the other hand, was determined that Herschel was not going to break the record. Tech battled back from a 17-0 deficit with a long touchdown drive in the fourth quarter to close the gap to 31-21. Tech was fired up and had the momentum after their fourth quarter touchdown. It lasted just a short time.

After returning the kickoff to the 35-yard line, it took only one play and a few seconds before the Bulldogs answered Tech's touchdown. Herschel went sixty-five yards. He broke the rushing record with a total of 1,616 yards and totally demoralized Tech's comeback thoughts. The play that broke the record was his favorite, the draw. We were on our 35 yard line, right hash mark. The call was "Slot Right Fly 24 Draw." The "fly" directed the flanker away from the formation. Tech's strong safety followed with him. The line blocking called for quick delay. The fullback, Ronnie Stewart, eliminated Tech's linebacker at the line of scrimmage. Herschel took a shuffle step left, got the ball from Buck and saw the hole open behind the fullback's block. Herschel broke a tackle at the line of scrimmage and ran away from everybody to the goal line. Herschel said that by the Tech game, "I had the confidence that even with angles they were not going to make tackles on me." There were three or four Tech defenders that had angles on Herschel but with his great speed he ran away from all of them.

There was nobody more proud of Herschel breaking Tony Dorsett's freshman rushing record than our offensive coordinator, George Haffner. George had coached Dorsett

at Pittsburgh when Tony set the freshman rushing record; with Herschel breaking Tony's record, it gave Haffner the distinction of coaching these two great backs when each player set the rushing record. It will be a lifetime point of pride for George.

The Bulldogs remained undefeated, 11-0, and were ranked No. 1. During the course of the season the rallying cry for each game became, "one more time."

The Sugar Bowl was next with the opportunity to become the first undefeated, undisputed national champions in Georgia's history. We told the team, "Somehow, someway, we've got to do it, one more time!"

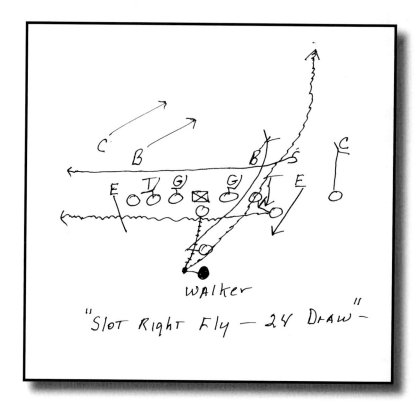

WALKER

"SloT RighT Fly — 24 DRAW —"

HERSCEL WALKER

VERSUS

NOTRE DAME

AT THE

SUGAR BOWL

JANUARY 1, 1981

"We always reminded our team: Expect the unexpected, anything can happen in a game. But, we were ready. . . ready to be national champions."

We were playing for the National Championship. This was an opportunity of a lifetime, and I knew the team was ready. Playing Notre Dame however was the ultimate challenge. The Irish were big, strong and quick. Their defense in particular was awesome. They ranked at the top nationally in every defensive category. No back had ever gained over 100 yards against their vaunted defense.

In spite of the challenge, we were ready. We always reminded our team of an old axiom: "Expect the unexpected, anything can happen in a game." We always told our team that regardless of what happens in the game, remain steady and keep fighting! That axiom came into focus on our second offensive play when Herschel Walker was hit out of bounds on a sweep and his shoulder was dislocated. He came to the sideline with his elbow in the air. He didn't say anything but that was Herschel. I knew that

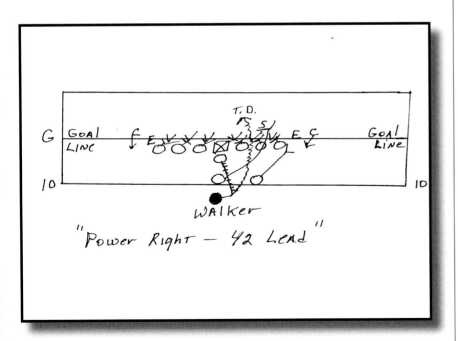

"Power Right — 42 Lead"

he was hurting. He went to the bench and our orthopedic physician, Dr. Butch Mulherin, put the dislocated shoulder back in place. Our trainer, Warren Morris, whom the players and coaches called 'Dr. Death,' told me, "Herschel is finished!" Warren always evaluated any injury in the worse possible way but his analysis was not what I wanted to hear. The news created an air of depression on our sidelines.

Herschel's mental and physical toughness overcame the injury and pain. When we next got the ball on offense, Herschel went back into the game. He said, "I didn't come all the way to New Orleans to play one or two plays." He played the rest of the game and gained 150 yards against the determined Notre Dame defense which had not given up 100 yards to any back the entire season. They were determined that Herschel would not gain 100 yards.

After we tied the score, 3-3, on a Rex Robinson field goal, Rex's ensuing kickoff, because of Notre Dame's miscommunication, was not fielded. It bounced on the artificial turf between the two returners. The Kelly brothers from Savannah, Steve and Bob, combined to recover the ball. Steve knocked the first Notre Dame player away from the football and Bob fell on the pigskin at the one-yard line. Man that was big!

As we had done numerous times throughout his career, we sent Herschel in and "over the top" to score. The touchdown put us up, 10-3. Throughout my career, there were two plays run by two players that I was one hundred percent confident would bring a score or a first down. The first was Ray Goff on the quarterback sneak. Ray was a big strong quarterback running behind an excellent offensive line and I believe he was one hundred percent successful on every one of his attempts. The other play was Herschel "over the top" and there are many classic pictures of him plunging up and over the pile.

He had incredible leaping ability. Some of his leaps against Florida were absolutely amazing. Herschel always said, "The adrenalin that he generated against the Gators was the highest." The touchdown leap that was replayed the most was against Ole Miss. He went high over the line and an Ole Miss linebacker stuck met him head-on and stood him up but Herschel rebounded off the defender, spinning in the air and coming down on his feet. He dashed into the end zone and politely handed the ball to the official. Herschel recalled the Ole Miss linebacker was trying to push him back but, "actually kept me balanced which allowed me to keep my feet and score." He said that he got many requests from the fans "to do it one more time."

I didn't realize it until later, but we put an extra strain on Herschel going over the top against Notre Dame. That dislocated shoulder, though back in place, was painful. We would forget that he was human, thinking that he would always perform like "superman!" Herschel said of the touchdown, "I didn't do my normal jump. I rolled away from my hurt shoulder and jumped at an angle to protect it. I didn't have to get up as high because the blocking was so good that it kept Notre Dame's defense low." I never knew that bit of information. However, after I saw the film, it was obvious that Herschel went over the top rolling on his right shoulder to protect his dislocated left shoulder.

We got another break early in the second period when Frank Ros, our captain, caused a Notre Dame fumble and Chris Welton recovered it at their 22-yard line. After big gains by Herschel and Buck Belue, Herschel swept right from the three for another touchdown. We were up, 17-3, at the half.

Notre Dame closed the gap in the third quarter with a touchdown to make it 17-10. We spent the rest of the fourth quarter fighting off Irish offensive thrusts. Scott Woerner intercepted his second pass of the day with 2:56 minutes left on the clock. The offense ran out the clock and the celebration of the national championship began. A wild sea of red cascaded onto the floor of the Super Dome, celebrating with memories to last a lifetime.

The 1980 team remains the closest of all the teams that I had the privilege of coaching. Certainly winning the national championship has a lot to do with that. Another important reason was the leadership of Frank Ros, our captain. Frank is the best captain we have ever had in my twenty-five years of coaching. He and his associates have kept this team close with ongoing personal contact and frequent reunions. There is no player that the team respected more. He was the classic over-achiever and one of the best conditioned football players I ever coached. During his career, he won the best conditioned athlete award every year. Herschel has the highest respect for Frank and they have remained close friends. Frank is very special to me and his leadership of the 1980 national championship team will be a very special memory of my career.

> "Hoage was one of the most remarkable players that I have ever had the privilege of coaching."

TERRY HOAGE
VERSUS
VANDERBILT UNIVERSTY
OCTOBER 15, 1983

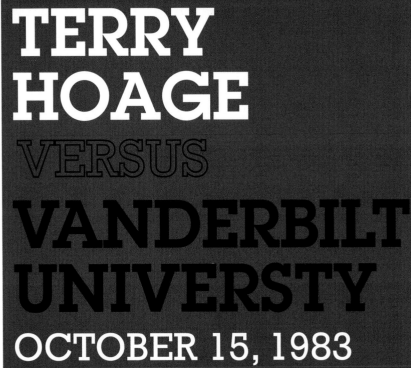

One of the most remarkable football players that I have ever had the privilege of coaching, Terry Hoage, made one of the most remarkable plays imaginable in my coaching career. Two time consensus All-American and Hall of Famer, Hoage was an extraordinary athlete and was equally extraordinary as a student. He made many remarkable plays in his career, but the one play he made in a night game against Vanderbilt in Nashville stands out as his greatest and most memorable.

Before reliving that incredible play which saved the game for us, it is important to travel the journey of Hoage's career as a Bulldog. The year we signed him to a scholarship ended up being the best recruiting class we ever had in my twenty-five years at Georgia. We signed the most sought after player in the country in Herschel Walker, and we signed the least sought after player in the country in Terry Hoage. Both became consensus All-Americans and members of the college football Hall of Fame.

In 1979 after signing a large share of those sought after players that we wanted, we had a couple of scholarships left. I instructed the staff to search for a couple of players who were good students with good character and determination to stay the course and perhaps help us in their junior or senior years.

Hoage was a high school quarterback who got hurt midway through his senior year of high school. His father was a college professor in Huntsville, Texas. Terry surely inherited his good genes and was an excellent student. He fit our criteria perfectly. However, when he finished his college career he far surpassed our greatest expectations. As a student Hoage became an Academic All-American compiling a 3.71 grade point average in genetics. He was a recipient of the two most prestigious academic awards in college sports: The NCAA Top Five Award Winner, given annually to the top five student athlete in any sport in the country. He was later inducted into the Academic All-American Hall of Fame.

His success as a football player parallels his extraordinary successes as a student. He led the nation in interceptions in 1982 with twelve. All American safety Jeff Sanchez was second in the nation in interceptions with nine. Between the two they had an amazing twenty-one interceptions in 1982. In 1983, Hoage blocked three field goals and had four quarterback sacks. He was named consensus All-American both years. He was later inducted into the College Football Hall of Fame and named by the Walter Camp Foundation to its All-Century Team. During the four years that he played at Georgia our record was 43-4-1, the best four year record of any team in the country.

We had planned to "red shirt" Hoage his freshman but he made me change my mind one day after the season during bowl practice. We were working full speed on field goals in preparation for Notre Dame for the national championship game in 1980. Hoage was on the scout team. He blocked three field goals against the kicking team in scrimmage. After the third block I told him to go inside and get packed. He was going to the Sugar Bowl and would start on the field goal blocking team. Interestingly, he blocked a Notre Dame field goal attempt which turned the momentum of the game in our favor as we beat the Irish to win the national championship.

Hoage and linebacker Ben Zambiazi were the two most relentless football player that I ever coached. This was true in practice and in games. The most memorable example of Hoage's relentlessness took place at night in Nashville his senior year in 1983.

We were ranked eighth in the country and heavily favored over an unranked Vanderbilt team. We were leading by a touchdown as the Commodores put together a last ditch effort and drove to our 24-yard line with less than a minute to play. Their quarterback, Kurt Page, lofted a pass to a wide open receiver in the back corner of the right end zone. Hoage who had tripped and fallen to the turf, was totally out of the play; however he made a miraculous recovery and with a spectacular leap got just enough of the middle finger of his right hand on the ball to deflect a certain touchdown pass. It was the most sensational play that I had ever seen. When I thought of all of the other incredible plays that he had made during his four year career, I didn't hesitate to call Hoage the best defensive player that I have ever coached.

Hoage remembered exactly what happened on the play. Vanderbilt was on the left hash mark on our 24-yard line and we were in a "man coverage" in the secondary. Hoage was locked-up with the inside receiver in Vanderbilt's formation which was a wide slot to the field. Hoage said, "The receiver ran a post and I jumped all over him, but he planted his foot and ran a post corner. I was completely faked out and I tripped, falling to the ground. I was embarrassed to let the team down and I told myself to get up and run wide open. The receiver was all alone in the end zone!" Hoage paid special tribute to Freddie Gilbert, "who flushed the quarterback out of the pocket and gave me enough time to recover." Hoage went flying in the air backwards and thanks to his long legs and arms he barely deflected the ball with the tip of his middle finger. Hoage said, "I was not sure that I touched the ball but perhaps I created enough wind velocity to deflect the ball."

When I told Hoage that his play against Vanderbilt was chosen as one of the thirty-four most memorable, he was surprised and said that he could think of many more plays that he made that in his mind were more important than the one in which he got faked out and fell to the ground. He is still embarrassed that he fell down that night in Nashville. Such a perfectionist! And to think, none of the Texas schools thought enough of him to offer him a scholarship.

Terry laughed, "I wonder about you coaches sometimes." He recalled a story when he was playing pro ball and one of his coaches emphasized another embarrassing moment. In the coach's mind it, too, was a highlight. Hoage said, "One year I was on special teams covering punts and as I came off the line of scrimmage to go downfield to cover the punt, I was 'decked' by a defensive linebacker. The defender literally ran over me. I quickly got up, raced down the field and made the tackle. Later during the film session, the coach kept running the film back and forth showing me getting knocked down and then getting up to make the tackle. I never thought he would stop showing me getting knocked down, which was very embarrassing."

I thought Terry's comments were revealing. It pointed out how coaches and players see things through different eyes. In Hoage's eyes it was an embarrassment to get knocked down or to trip and fall down as he did in the Vanderbilt game. In the coach's eye many players get knocked down or fall but the champions and winners are those that get up in a hurry and do something about it. I though Hoage's play in the Vanderbilt game was a great lesson on the football field and also in life. His example is why I thought the play was extraordinary and memorable. Obviously his NFL coach thought his tackle, after being knocked down, was likewise a great teaching example.

After college Hoage played thirteen years career in the NFL. When his playing days were over, he began growing grapes in Paso Robles, California. Today he is a very successful wine maker. His most successful wine product was named "The Hedge," as a special tribute to his career at Georgia where he made so many memorable plays "between the hedges." The "Hedge" is a classic, just like the play he made in Nashville the night of October 15, 1983.

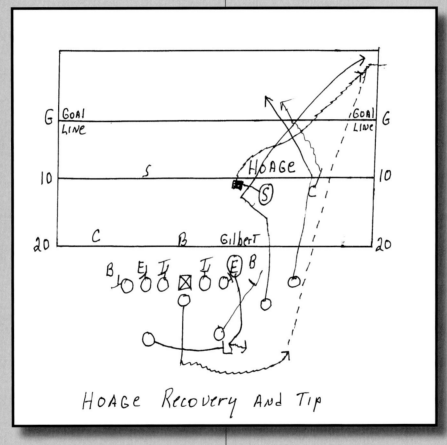

HOAGE Recovery And Tip

JOHN LATSINGER
VERSUS
UNIVERSITY
OF TEXAS
JANUARY 1, 1984

John Lastinger called his last play as a Bulldog "One of those Glory Glory to 'Ol Georgia moments." He ran 17 yards for the go ahead touchdown with 3:22 left on the clock in the Cotton Bowl which enabled us to defeat No. 2 ranked Texas, 10-9. Before that glorious moment, Lastinger had a series of ups with a lot of downs in his career as a Bulldog quarterback. The Cotton Bowl, until the end, was just as frustrating for Lastinger.

John was one of the genuinely nicest young men I had the privilege to coach. He was an excellent athlete but his only problem was that he lacked the confidence that normally is associated with playing quarterback. When Buck Belue was the quarterback at Valdosta High School, Lastinger was a wide receiver and cherished that role. When Buck left for Georgia Lastinger reluctantly agreed to play quarterback but proceeded to lead Valdosta to the state championship game.

At Georgia, John started at defensive back, but was shifted to quarterback behind Belue. He suffered an injured knee and was redshirted for the 1980 season. That

was the beginning of a series of frustrating knee injuries. He re-injured his knee in the spring, but recovered in time to start at quarterback after Belue left following the 1981 season. In 1982, Lastinger's performance was excellent at times but at times inconsistent. However he finished strong to lead our team to the SEC title and into the Sugar Bowl with an 11-0 record and a NO. 1 ranking. The opponent was Penn State, ranked NO. 2. Lastinger played well enough for us to win, but Penn state edged us late in the game to win, 27-23.

Despite the loss of Herschel, who left early, we had a solid team in 1983 and were optimistic about Lastinger leading the team. He was a great competitor with very good leadership qualities. His confidence was growing. Midway through spring practice, disaster struck again as Lastinger injured his other knee! We were discouraged, thinking that we could not count on him in the fall. He was initially more discouraged than we were and said he wasn't sure if he "had the motivation to come back again."

Thanks to Valdosta State's trainer Jim Madaleno, John went through rehabilitation and returned to Athens in August in top shape. Madaleno worked at challenging Lastinger all summer while he was in Valdosta. While Lastinger's knee recovered nicely with Madaleno's rehab program, Lastinger's lack of attention to quarterback drills hurt him early in the year. Thanks to Todd Williams, John's back-up, we kept winning. We played both quarterbacks. Toward the end of the season Lastinger caught fire, his greatest moment coming against Florida in the fourth quarter when he directed a 99-yard fourth quarter drive to edge Florida, 10-9.

We were beaten the next week by a really good Auburn team (13-7) snapping our twenty-three game SEC win streak. It also denied up a fourth consecutive SEC championship. We didn't go down easily, however. We rallied late in the game and almost pulled it out under Lastinger's superb leadership.

We beat Tech and accepted a bid to to the Cotton Bowl to play No. 2 ranked Texas. Playing Texas was a tremendous challenge. Their defense would ranl at the top of the great defensive teams that we faced in my twenty-five years at Georgia. Eight of their eleven starters were NFL draft picks. However, their offense was average, and I felt that if we played sound football and hung tough with them that we had a good chance of winning.

Texas's defense was even better than we thought. At the end of the game we had only 215 yards of total offense. Late in the fourth quarter we had scored only three points. The good news was that Texas only had scored only nine. It was imperative to maintain the positive spirits of Lastinger and our offense alive. After being frustrated time and time again, we were still within striking distance if we could create an opportunity. The break came when Gary Moss recovered a fumbled punt at the Texas 23-yard line with 4:30 minutes left in the game.

We ran two plays that netted us only six yards and it looked as if the Texas defense was going to hold as they had done all game. However, those two plays helped to set up Lastinger's touchdown. One of the plays was a handoff to tailback Tron Jackson and was run from a flanker motion set. Herman Archie was our flanker and their cornerback, playing tough man coverage, focused on Archie. This created an opportunity for an option to the back side which was spotted by our coaches in the press box. The other play was "54," a reverse hand off to our fullback. On Lastinger's run, he faked to the fullback which drew the focus of the Texas offense. Lastinger made a terrific fake, kept the ball and dived into the end zone, right over the boundary pylon.

I thought that we needed to throw the ball, but ofensive coordinator George Haffner and our offensive line coach Alex Gibbs thought that the option was there. Thank goodness we went with it: "Flanker Right Motion 54 Option." Lastinger faked to our fullback Barry Young and got an effective "brush block" from him on the weak side linebacker. He also got a great block from Guy McIntyre on the strong side linebacker. Clarence Kay had an excellent block on their defensive end. Lastinger then had to read the strong safety to determine if he was going to take the quarterback or the pitch man, Tron Jackson. Since they were playing man in the secondary, the strong safety took Jackson and Lastinger recalled that "for a split second I saw an opening to the goal line." It was a race between their safety and Lastinger for the pylon. Lastinger thought to himself, "Lord please let me get there first." He won the race and when he looked up he saw the official "had his arms raised in the air." I asked Lastinger if he remembered who we had in the game at tailback and he said, "Absolutely. It was Tron Jackson who kept shouting "pitch it to me, pitch it to me, which I ignored."

Kevin Butler kicked the extra point to make it 10-9. Texas still had time but a couple of sacks finished them off as we took control and ran off the final 2:19 of the clock after making a first down at the Texas 37-yard line.

That night Miami beat the NO. 1 Nebraska in the Orange Bowl. Nebraska's defeat would have given Texas the national championship had they beaten Georgia, but Lastinger's "Glory, Glory moment" denied Texas their opportunity to reach the top of the college football world. That moment in time Lastinger said, "Erased all the bad stuff that happened in my career." It also provided him and the Bulldog nation with a memory that they will relish for a life time. For sure the time for Georgia fans will always be 10-9 in Texas!

"For Georgia fans the time in Texas will always be 10-9! It was one of those 'Glory, Glory to 'Ol Georgia' moments."

"Right - Motion 54 Option"

KEVIN BUTLER VERSUS CLEMSON UNIVERSITY

SEPTEMBER 22, 1984

Kevin Butler was not only Georgia's greatest kicker, he was arguable the greatest kicker n college football history. Of the thousand-plus college football players inducted into the Hall of Fame, Butler is the only field goal kicker to ever been selected. Kevin was a four-time, All-SEC selection and a two-time consensus All American. Butler has received numerous honors but a few honors are especially distinctive and worth underscoring. He was named to the All-Country team selected by Walter Camp Football Foundation and *Sports Illustrated*. He was also selected by ABC Sports to the college Football All-Time, All-American Team. After college, he kicked in the NFL

for twelve years, setting numerous Chicago Bears club and NFL records.

Butler's name is listed near the top of most every place kicking category at Georgia, the SEC and the NCAA. His long field goal kicks separate him from all of the other great kickers at Georgia. Butler kicked eleven field goals over fifty yards in his career including kicks of 57, 59, and 60 yards. He was such a fierce competitor with supreme confidence that every time that we got past mid-field, he would make his presence known to me on the side lines. At times he would walk back and forth in front of me with his head gear on looking right at me. There were several occasions that I had to push him out of the way since I was more interested in our team scoring touchdowns and was totally involved in seeing that we put the ball in the end-zone. In Kevin's mind, however, he was reminding me that he was available!

It is appropriate to pay tribute to Kevin's kicking coach the late and beloved, Coach Bill Hartman. Coach Hartman coached Bulldog kickers for twenty one years. He was among the handful of people who remained a loyal friend and supporter throughout my forty plus years at Georgia. He was a great confidante. Coach Hartman had the ideal personality for a kicking coach. The kickers loved him for his patient and calm demeanor, and I am sure of the kickers would echo what Butler had to say about him. "When you talk about kicking, you talk about Bill Hartman when you come from Georgia. He was really the first person who led me down the right road to kicking. He taught me the fundamentals of kicking and turned the physical part of kicking into a mental game. That is what Coach Hartman did best. He created a good relaxed, positive feeling when I went out on the field." I would be remiss prior to reliving Butler's record setting 60-yard kick if I didn't mention his kicking heroics in the

Clemson and BYU games of 1982. Butler had kicked a couple of field goals in our 13-7 win over Clemson in our opening game that year on national television. The game was played in primetime on Labor Day 1982, pitting the 1980 national champions (Georgia) against 1981 national champions (Clemson).

The game was not over until early Tuesday which gave us an extremely short week and difficult task of preparing for an excellent BYU team the following Saturday. The game was tied, 14-14, and we had a late minute drive that got us in field goal range with 1:11 minutes left on the clock. Butler kicked a 44-yard field goal that enabled Georgia to defeat BYU, 17-14. The Bulldogs went on to finish the season undefeated, winning the SEC championship for the third time in a row. We then lost to Penn State in the Sugar Bowl for the national championship. It still grinds on me!

When it comes to Butler's career, the game that everyone likes to talk about is his 60-yard field goal to beat Clemson. The kick still stands as an SEC record (tied) today.

In 1984, Clemson came to Athens ranked No. 2 in the nation and highly favored. They lived up to their ranking in the first half and had us down, 20-6. Butler remembered that I was not happy at half time, "not because we were losing but because we were playing so lethargically."

We fought back and tied the score, 20-20, at the end of the third quarter. We swapped field goals in the fourth quarter. With the score 23-23, we had one final drive that reached Clemson's 43-yard line. I never hesitated in sending Butler in to kick. I had seen him kick sixty yards and more on many occasions in practice. Butler said: "I had confidence in myself, but it freaked out the people in the stands that we would attempt from that distance. When it

left my foot I knew that I had hit it solid. I watched it for a second to make sure it was going to maintain its course. I remember looking at my holder, Jimmy Harrell, and seeing that smile on his face as the ball sailed through. Then I raced toward the student section and dropped to my knees." When Kevin first started running in that direction I thought that he was heading toward the cheerleaders to embrace his girlfriend, Cathy, who became his wife. Maybe he thought better of the idea since we still had eleven seconds left in the game.

The kicked cleared the crossbar with enough lift that it could have gone seventy yards, which is why I never hesitated to put Kevin in to try a 72-yarder against Florida State in the Citrus Bowl to break a 17-17 tie. The kick was true but fell a yard short! I am still mad today that we did not do a good job of play selection that could have gotten us a couple of yards closer. However the score board clock broke and the time was kept on the field by the officials. This added to our poor clock management. Had we done a better job, Butler would be holding a field goal record that probably would never be broken. Nevertheless, his SEC record 60-yarder game winner to beat the Clemson Tigers till remains the most famous kick in Georgia's football history.

"Of the thousand-plus college football players inducted into the Hall of Fame, Butler is the only field goal kicker to ever been selected."

RICHARD TARDITS

VERSUS
TEXAS CHRISTIAN UNIVERSITY

SEPTEMBER 10, 1988

Prior to spring practice in 1985 I was told that a walk-on from France, who had never even seen an American football game wanted to come out for our team. I was somewhat amused and naturally dubious but welcomed this fellow named Richard Tardits from Biarritz, France. Naturally, the question our friend immediately faced was: why would he want to take on such a daunting challenge. Watching Tardits in those early days of spring practice confirmed that he knew absolutely nothing about the game. However, it was also apparent that he was a fine athlete, a very good physical specimen with speed. Equally important, he was tenacious, intelligent and had a marvelous attitude. He was wager to learn the game. We knew that it would be a difficult process, but if he was willing to stick with it we welcomed him aboard.

Along the way we had a few good- natured laughs about his French accent, his foreign mannerisms, and his football miscues. However, we soon forgot about his goals to make the team as we turned out attention to getting prepared for the season. Tardits, however, refused to let us ignore him. As a scout team defensive player, he displayed a natural and uncanny ability to rush the passer.

In a Sanford Stadium scrimmage in the fall he sacked our quarterback five times. After the fifth sack I gave him a "battle field promotion," awarding him a scholarship on the spot. I will never forget his reaction. He jumped off of the ground, stood in front of me at attention. I thought that he was going to salute. In his charming French accent said, "Thank you very much coach!"

Initially, we used him strictly as a pass rushing specialist. With experience, he soon developed the knack of being an all-around defensive player. To the amazement of all, he became an All-SEC player, leading the conference in quarterback sacks. He was drafted in the fourth round by the Arizona Cardinals and played five years of professional football. An ankle injury cut short his playing career in 1992.

Tardit's uncanny ability to rush the passer earned him the nickname, "Le Sack." His twenty-nine career sacks were a Georgia record which stood for sixteen years until broken by three time All-American David Pollack.

The Richard Tardits story is the most amazing in college football and certainly the most memorable in my experience. If ever there was a "Renaissance Man," it was Richard. He was an excellent student finishing his undergraduate degree prior to the start of his senior year. He went on to earn a MBA in international business. He was awarded an NCAA post-graduate scholarship.

He endeavored to experience everything life had to offer. He ran with the bulls in Pamplona, Spain and played rugby in his hometown in Biarritz, France, with aspirations to play with a New Zealand team. At Georgia he participated in many activities available on the Georgia campus. I often saw him zipping around campus on a skate board, a sport he enjoyed with uncanny efficiency.

After his career in the NFL, he started an environmental business in Atlanta and became ver successful. After marrying a lovely English lady, JoAnna, he sold his business and they moved back to his hometown in Biarritz, France to raise their children: Charlotte, Sam, and Elodie. Barbara and I had a lovely visit with the family in their sea coast chateau. We also saw the magnificent golf course he is developing in the resort town of Bigorre at the foot of the snow-covered Pyrenees mountains. He is a licensed French pilot, he surfs in the Atlantic Ocean near his home, and plays Rugby on the local team.

Tarditis' most remarkable game was against TCU in 1988, his senior year. He had ten tackles (seven solo), four quarterback sacks and graded an amazing ninety-five percent. But his most memorable plays came on back-to-back quarterback sacks. The sacks came when TCU was threatening to get back into the game. We dominated the game early on and were leading, 14-3, when TCU mounted a good drive to mid-field. The threat was thwarted after Tardits made his sacks, forcing the Horn Frogs to punt from their own 28-yard line.

After the TCU punt, Georgia had good field position around the 50-yard line. We scored in two plays. Quarterback Greg Talley hit wide receiver Arthur Marshall for forty yards at the TCU nine-yard line. On the next play, Tim Worley, on a half-back pass, hit tight end Troy Sadowski for a touchdown and we were up, 21-3. From that point on we coasted to an easy 38-10 victory.

The TCU coach, Jim Wacker and the Horn Frogs's quarterback Scott Anatom, was amazed at Tardits' performance. Coach Wacker called Tardits "The number one pass rusher in the country." Anaron said, "My god No. 92, and he is the best I have ever seen especially since he has been playing football only four years. Unbelievable!" After the game, Tardits acquired another nickname: The Biarritz Blitz.

Re-living Tardits' performance stirred my memory of his unique pass rushing technique. I called his route to the quarterback, the "Tour de France," because of its unusual course. With his incredible starting speed, Tardits would run around the blocker at the corner, head "north," going all the way around the offense, then turn and head back "south" coming in on the quarterback from the rear. I was quoted as saying, "It took a long way around to get there but he always got his man!"

The "Tour de France" route of "Le Sack" especially in the TCU game will always be among my most memorable plays. However there is far more to enjoy about the "Biarritz Blitz" so I am including the response by Tardits to some questions that I asked him in writing this chapter. His responses provide a humorous insight into his American adventure and provide a marvelous testimony to the value of an American education both in the classroom and on the gridiron.

What drove you to play football at Georgia?

"While staying in Augusta for a month through a family exchange program, I learned about the American University system and the great opportunity for a young person to achieve high academic results while being sponsored (scholarship) to participate in the greatest amateur sport organization in the world the NCAA. I stayed with Dr. Edward Servy, a professor at the Augusta Medical College, and he introduced me to his friend Dr. Mixon Robinson, the Georgia Team Orthopedic who had earlier played for the Bulldogs. Dr. Robinson, familiar with the skills required in rugby, encouraged me to walk on at Georgia. I decided to walk on with the intent of earning a scholarship and an MBA degree.

How did you learn to put on the uniform?

My first practice (spring of 1985) was truly a christening of football since I had to learn the game and, more, the simple act of putting on the uniform. Too proud to ask, I decided to look around in the locker room and to do exactly as the other players were doing. The plan almost worked, except I hadn't noticed that inside the football pants were special pockets to insert knee, thigh and tailbone pads. I just stuck the pads in my pants thinking everything would be okay. Within a few steps on the practice field, the pads were falling out of my pants. Thank God, a team manager named Jojo (Walker) saw me and wondered if my pants were torn and didn't have the special pockets. I had to take my pants off while everyone was watching and finally learned how to dress like a football player. Even though embarrassing, it was not as bad as the bruising "bull in the ring" drill you do as a defensive player. I had no idea how it worked, and once again, too embarrassed to ask, I just watched and thought it wasn't that hard. When one of the players pointed at me. I stepped forward nonchalantly and was hit right under the chin, thus giving me my first knockout in American football. What were your thoughts when you were given the "battlefield" promotion (scholarship) after you had five sacks in a stadium scrimmage?

"If you recall, we had a meeting before summer camp in 1985. I asked what the chances were of me getting a football scholarship. I don't know why you didn't laugh at this request, especially when I realized years later how many young football players were dreaming about a scholarship to play ball for the Dawgs. You very sincerely told me about the difficulty of the task, but you also told

"The Richard Tardits story is the most amazing in college football and certainly the most memorable in my experience."

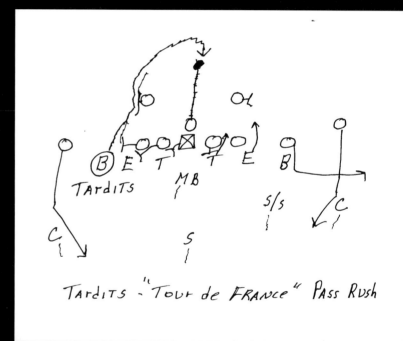

TArdiTs - "Tour de FRANce" PAss RUsh

me that if I could make myself instrumental in helping the team win, you would evaluate my situation after the season. No more needed to be said. I knew I at least had a chance.

The big break came when Greg Waters, the top rusher on the team, was injured. You needed a pass rusher. During tryouts at the end of a practice, I was selected among others to be a candidate. I'll never forget the scrimmage at Sanford Stadium. While playing against the first offense, I was able, many times, to get into the backfield and either pressure or sack Todd Williams, the starting quarterback. At one point after another sack, you came over the help me up from the turf said: 'You don't have to wait until the end of the year to be a part of our team, you earned your scholarship today!' I couldn't wait to get off the field to telephone my parents with the news. I was relieved not to be a financial burden any longer, especially since I made the choice I had made for myself to try as Georgia, giving up free tuition in the French educational system. I felt as an adult; I could take care of myself.

Early on, you were a great pass rusher. Recall your experience of growing from pass rushing specialist to becoming a complete player.

One of the things I took from the game of rugby, which I had played all my life in France, was the ability to avoid people, not be tackled, which translated in not being blocked. My strategy, which you called "the Tour de France Technique," was to explode off the ball and run around the blocker instead of trying to rush through him. Most offensive tackles expected to be "bull" rushed, having the defensive linemen come straight ahead, driving you back. Having greater quickness than they, my objective was to freeze them and run around them. The only drawback was the hole it created behind me. We had

excellent inside linebackers like Billy Mitchell, Steve Boswell, and John Brantley who covered for me. With extra time on the field, I learned the intricacies of the running game and the coverage game to become a fulltime linebacker. I must say that rushing the passer was the most exciting thing about football to me. I really felt that I had an impact on the game.

What are your other thoughts about your experiences?

The American university system provides the greatest opportunity for a young person to develop, especially if the financial burden is removed by a scholarship. Being able to shoot for the stars both in your academic career and in your athletic career is the best that anyone could ask for. It is sad that many of the young football players don't understand that and do not take advantage of the great opportunity that is available to them. The values taught in the game of football—discipline, respect and, persistence—are the basic ones for success in life.

MIKE BOBO
TO COREY
ALLEN
VERSUS
AUBURN
UNIVERSITY
NOVEMBER 16, 1996

It was the 100th meeting between Georgia and Auburn when the two teams met in 1996 at Jordan-Hare Stadium in Auburn, Alabama. The Bulldogs beat the Tigers that night, 56-49, in a classic that might well be the wildest game ever played between these old rivals. To settle the game, four over-times were required. It was the longest in SEC history. There were numerous remarkable twists and turns in the contest. The most memorable of these came with one second left when quarterback Mike Bobo heaved a 30-yard touchdown pass to Corey Allen who out-jumped the Auburn defender to send the game into overtime. Prior to that incredible play there were many other dramatics that took place, before and during the game.

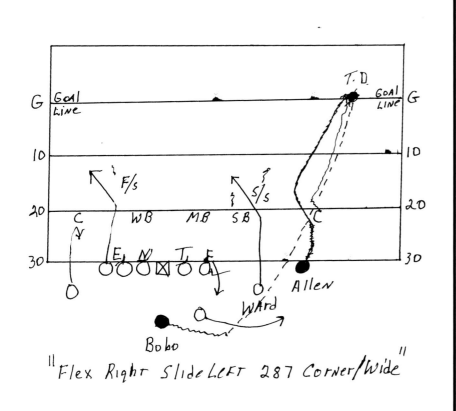

"Flex Right Slide Left 287 Corner/Wide"

Coach Jim Donnan's first Georgia team had its worst record after eight games (3-5) in thirty-five years. The Dawgs were playing a nationally ranked team. After a humiliating lost to Florida, 47-7, in the previous game, Coach Donnan, in an unusual move, decided not to start quarterback Mike Bobo and running back Robert Edwards. The move designed to take pressure off of the pair, especially since they had committed too many turnovers in the Florida game the week before. It proved to be a very wise decision as both came off of the bench to become heroes.

Bobo entered the game with Georgia down 28-7 and led the team to two touchdowns late in the game. Most of the yardage in the two scoring drives was accounted for by future Pittsburgh Steelers' Super Bowl MVP, Hines Ward, who had a total of 251 total yards in the game.

Bobo, who connected on twenty-one of thirty-seven passes for 360 yards and two touchdowns, led the team on an amazing 82-yard drive with no time outs in the final 1:07 minutes of playing time. With a few seconds left on the clock, Bobo was sacked and the game probably would have ended there since Georgia had no time outs left. Thanks, however, to an Auburn defensive lineman who picked up the ball after the sack and started running with it gave Georgia a last ray of hope. The official had to stop the clock to retrieve the ball. Bobo said, "This enabled us to quickly line up and execute the 'clock play' stopping the clock with one second left." Bobo described in detail exactly what happened on the big play that was called, "Flex Right Slide Left 287 Corner/Wide." "Flex Right" was the formation. "Slide Left" indicated the blocking. The number 287 designated the routes: corner the route of the tight-end, wide the respective route of the running backs.

"They were playing a soft quarters coverage," Bobo remembers. Coach Donnan diagramed the play to hit Hines Ward down the middle. We had the backside tight-end run a flag route to hold the free-safety and then try to hit Hines down the middle against their "cover 2" alignment. This means the cornerbacks would normally play tight coverage.

"At the snap they were playing soft, not 'cover 2' as we had anticipated. Evidently, they were playing soft (deep) because it was the last play of the game. The line-backers played underneath and covered the post route by Hines. The backside free safety cheated to the field. After the snap, I saw the middle of the field was covered which meant I could not go to Hines, but I knew Corey Allen would be one-on-one to the outside, with Auburn's corner. I had a little pressure by the defensive end and I had to step to the right. I looked inside to hold the strong safety, then I threw it up to Corey Allen who definitely had the defensive back one on one. Corey made a great catch at the goal line and fell into the end zone for the touchdown."

After Allen's sensational catch, Hap Hines kicked the extra point tying the score, 28-28, sending the game into overtime. It took four overtimes before Georgia finally prevailed, 56-49. The Bobo-to-Allen last second pass would not have been so significant had the Dawgs lost to Auburn. Thanks primarily to the heroics of Robert Edwards, who came off the bench to account for ninety-seven of Georgia's 100 yards and three of the Bulldogs' four touchdowns in overtime, Bobo-to-Allen is one of Georgia's thirty-four most memorable plays.

"With one second left, Bobo heaved a 30-yard touchdown to tie the game. The Bulldogs won after four dramatic overtimes."

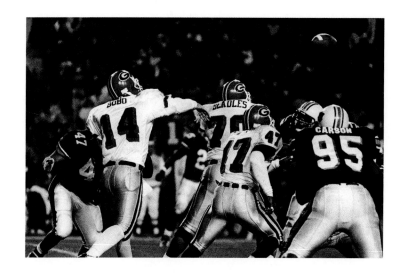

MIKE BOBO TO COREY ALLEN

NOVEMBER 29, 1997 VERSUS GEORGIA TECH

The 1997 Georgia-Georgia Tech game was another classic in the great tradition of these ancient state rivals. Georgia Tech went up, 24-21, with 48 seconds left in the game and appeared to have broken Georgia's victory streak of six game. Instead Georgia stormed down the field with quarterback Mike Bobo connecting with Corey Allen deep in the endzone for an eight yard touchdown with seven seconds left to win the game—a memorable drive capped by a memorable play.

Georgia had dominated play early and held a solid 21-10 lead. Tech fought back and scored two touchdowns, the last one coming with 48 seconds left, giving Tech a 22-21 advantage. Georgia Tech converted the two point play and went up, 24-21, apparently sending the Bulldogs down to defeat.

Tech mistakenly kicked off out of bounds and Georgia got the ball on its own 35-yard line. This favorable break took no time off the clock. On the first play Bobo hit "60-minute man" Champ Bailey on a tunnel screen for twenty-eight yards and then hit Bailey again for seven yards. On the next play, Bobo passed to Robert Edwards for nine and Georgia had a first and ten opportunity on Tech's 21-yard line, with twenty-one seconds left.

The next play was really big. Coach Donnan wanted to get the ball in the hands of Hines Ward who was lined up in a slot to the left side of the field. The play was designed to take advantage of the alignment of two safeties in Tech's "cover 2" defense. This, he correctly assumed, would enable Bobo to connect with Ward down the middle of the safeties. Tech's strong safety, Travis Tillman stepped in front of Ward and intercepted the ball. To the sheer delight of the Tech fans, it appeared that once again it was all over for the Bulldogs. Suddenly, a flag brought hope. Everyone assumed that the official had called pass interference on the strong safety who had made a great play to intercept Bobo's pass. The Tech fans understandably went bonkers. However the ruling was not pass interference, but holding by the Tech linebacker who grabbed Ward as he released past the line of scrimmage.

Georgia Tech's Coach, George O'Leary, was livid with the call and demanded an explanation. During the official time out to explain the call, Bobo said he went to the sidelines to discuss the next play with Coach Donnan.

Bobo said, "I told him the safety was not getting off of the hash and we could hit Allen in the hole in their cover 2. Coach said, run it!"

After play was resumed, the penalty gave the Bulldogs a first down on Tech's eight yard line with approximately twelve seconds left. In the middle, Bobo calmly called "Flex Left QK Slide Right 989 Block/Block." "Flex" left was the formation, "QK slide right" meant quick line protection, "right" meant aggressive, "989" referred to the routes of the three wide receivers.

"At the snap of the ball," Bobo recalled, "I looked at Hines, which made the focus on Hines, and threw a 'wobbly duck' in the corner of the end-zone to Corey Allen. The Tech corner thought he had help from the strong safety and didn't drop in 'cover 2' fast enough."

Bobo to Allen's 8-yard touchdown pass gave Georgia the victory and the seventh consecutive win over Georgia Tech. It was a miserable ending for Tech and a glorious ending for the Bulldogs thanks to a fortuitous development and keen execution by Bobo and Allen.

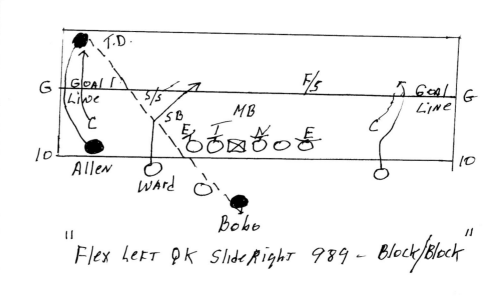

"Flex Left QK SlideRight 989 - Block/Block"

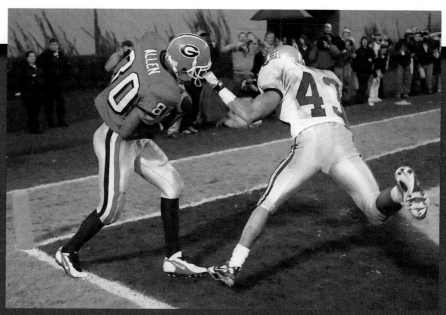

"Tech was up 24-21 with 48 seconds left and was about to break Georgia's six game winning streak. when Georgia stormed down the field"

New head coach Mark Richt and freshman quarterback David Greene led the Bulldogs into hostile Neyland Stadium hosted by sixth-ranked Tennessee. The Volunteers led, 14-3, in the second quarter but Georgia fought back and went ahead, 20-17, on Billy Bennett's 31-yard field goal. After an interception by the Bulldogs late in the game the score looked safe. However, Georgia was forced to punt with a minute left to play. Then, like a cannon shot, Tennessee's Travis Stephens took a screen pass and raced sixty-two yards for a touchdown and a 24-20 lead with 44 seconds remaining in the game. Most all the 107,592 in attendance went "bananas" and it appeared that the highly ranked Volunteers had pulled it out in the last seconds.

But Tennessee, who dominated the Dawgs in the nineties winning nine of the previous ten games, had not faced this new brand of Bulldogs under rookie head coach Mark Richt. The new coach's theme of "finish the drill," caught fire in Bulldog country. Nor had Tennessee faced a freshman quarterback like David Greene whose calm demeanor would start a string of victories unequaled by a quarterback in Bulldog, SEC and NCAA history. Greene eventually won more football games (forty-two) than any quarterback in the history of the game and still, to date, holds the NCCA record.

After Tennessee's last second touchdown, the Vols decided to kick the ball flat, thus trying to avoid a long kick-off return. The call backfired on them. The ball went a short distance enabling Georgia to start the drive from their 41-yard line. Flanker Damien Gary caught a Greene pass for a thirteen yard gain and tight end Randy McMichaels caught two for twenty-six and fourteen yards. In four plays Greene had Georgia on Tennessee's 6-yard

DAVID GREENE TO VERRON HAYNES VERSUS TENNESSEE
OCTOBER 6, 2001

line. With ten seconds left on the clock, Georgia called time out and Greene and the receiving corps came to the sidelines for a conference with Coach Richt.

Coach Richt called "right flex P-44 Haynes," a great percentage call. "right flex" (the formation), "P-44" (fake the running play to the tailback), "Haynes" (the fullback receiver).

"Eighty percent of the time Tennessee's secondary had been in 'quarter coverage' in the red zone and the play was designed especially for that coverage," said Greene. However in case Tennessee was not in quarterback coverage, Coach Richt instructed Greene "to throw it away quickly and he would decide what to call on the next play." "P-44 Haynes" was named after Verron Haynes the personable and outgoing fullback who 'walked on' and became famous by catching the pass for the winning touchdown. Haynes recalled that "we practiced the play each week. Coach Richt brought the play from FSU and Greene recalls Coach Richt telling him that it was called, "P-44 Hank," obviously after a former fullback for the Seminoles.

It will always be called "P-44-Haynes" at Georgia. However another inspiring walk-on fullback, J.T. Wall caught the same pass play for a touchdown the following year against Florida in the opening drive, but Haynes humorously said that they didn't change the play to "P-44 Wall."

Both Greene and Haynes said that Coach Richt told them on the sidelines, during the time out, that the play will be either a "penthouse or an outhouse" play. Coach Richt doesn't recall using that expression which is an often used phrase in the coaching profession. The saying refers to how fast a coach and or a team can go from the mountain top to the pits or from the "penthouse to the outhouse," or vice versa in a season, a game or even a play.

All coaches have experienced that roller coaster ride, but former Georgia Tech coach, my friend Pepper Rogers, is the only coach that went from the "White House to the outhouse." One night he was in Washington having dinner with then President Jimmy Carter at the White House and when he got back home to Atlanta, the very next day, he was fired! Nevertheless, coaches often forget what they say to the players or to the team but the players never forget.

Haynes said when Coach Richt called the play, "I was a nervous wreck. When I lined up prior to the snap, I could see they were in Quarters. I told myself over and over again, 'catch the ball, catch the ball' ... that was the longest five seconds of my career." Coach Mike Bobo, the quarterback coach, who was in the press box, said he "knew it was there if Haynes could get through the line clean and avoid the linebacker." Haynes told me he went at the linebacker like he had done all day blocking for Musa Smith on the lead play, and "at the last second I slipped by him and I was all alone." Bobo further explained in the diagram of the play, "The wide receivers had run corner routes to influence the safeties to double them leaving the fullback one on one with the mike linebacker." Greene play-faked to the tailback to encourage the linebackers to step up and then flipped the ball to Haynes who 'looked it in' and the Bulldogs went ahead, 26-24, with five seconds left in the game.

The Bulldogs at the game went wild with excitement. The rest of the Bulldog nation that were listening on the radio, were close to hysteria especially after hearing Munson say, "We just crushed their face with a Hob Nail Boot"!

Haynes ran off the field with the football to the bench and his teammates swarmed him. He told me that in all the celebration he lost the ball on the sidelines and he never found it especially since he was ordered back in the game for the extra point.   It is a shame that Verron does not have the football he caught that made him eternally famous in the Bulldog nation.   However, he does have that memorable play to his credit that will always be named after him.

It is truly an inspiring story! A "walk-on" catches a dramatic last second touchdown pass against a great conference rival using a play that is now named after him. Besides playing several years of pro ball that walk-on Verron (P-44) Haynes earned a Super bowl ring while playing with the Washington Redskins to top off a string of inspiring memories for a lifetime!

"A 'walk-on' catches a last second touchdown pass using a play now named after him. Haynes' story is truly inspiring."

"Right Flex P44 Haynes"

DAVID POLLACK

VERSUS

UNIVERSITY OF SOUTH CAROLINA

SEPTEMBER 14, 2002

"Great plays on defense are made by great players because they are characteristically relentless in their pursuit of the football."

After losing two in a row to South Carolina, ninth ranked Georgia was facing the Gamecocks in Columbia with energized anticipation. It would always be a challenge playing South Carolina early in the season, especially in Columbia. The Bulldogs wanted to avoid losing three straight in a row to the Gamecocks for the first time ever in the history of the long series.

Playing during the tropical storm "Hanna," the game turned into a defensive struggle with the only points scored in the first three quarters coming from the Bulldogs' kicker, Billy Bennett's field goal.

Early in the fourth quarter, the Gamecocks were backed up on their own 5-yard line when David Pollack made one of the most extraordinary defensive plays that I have ever seen in all my years involved with college football.

Pollack's play against South Carolina was ranked No. 3 among the all-time best, top fifty College Football plays on ESPN's "The Best Damn Sports Show." I would like to know where Pollack's play was ranked defensively. Most of the fifty greatest plays chosen were offensive plays, like Boston College's Doug Flutie's "Hail Mary" against Miami in 1984. There were other dramatic last second touchdowns, including the famous multiple lateral touch-down on a kick-off return by California against Stanford. I would be remiss not to mention the Cal player running over the tuba player when the Stanford band took the field too early for the victory celebration.

Pollack recalls exactly what happened on his miraculous play that scored the only touchdown of the game in the 13-10 victory in Columbia. "I was lined up outside of South Carolina's right tackle, in Georgia's base defense. "The Gamecocks came to the line of scrimmage in 'trips' to my side." Pollack was referring to an offensive formation where three receivers line up to one side of the field. Based on the scouting report, South Carolina "often rolled in that formation to the trips side." Pollack, anticipating the play, "got a good jump and beat the tackle." He then engaged

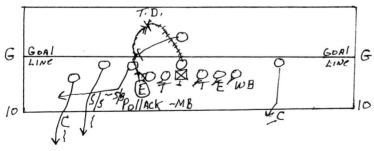

Pollack Quarter Back Strip - T.D

the back who was trying to chip him or block him around his ankles. After eliminating the second blocker, Pollack tried to "square up," on the quarterback Corey Jenkins to "block his view or hit the ball. As he jumped, I hit his arm and as I was falling behind him I saw the ball almost rolling down his back and I grabbed it." The official was in "perfect position to see the play and when he signaled touchdown I went nuts!" When Pollack went "nuts," the team went "nuts" too, celebrating long before the stunned crowd knew what had happened.

The touchdown was the most dramatic of many great plays made by Pollack. Great plays on defense are made by great players because they are characteristically relentless in their pursuit of the football. The only other player at Georgia that compares to Pollack in his dogged pursuit of the football was the two time All-American and Hall of Famer Terry Hogue. Pollack is a three time All-American, the first one since Herschel Walker and will surely be inducted into the Football College Hall of Fame, as soon as he becomes eligible.

Pollack's play was a defensive "Statue of Liberty" play. Pollack was now in a class of his own in a career of making big plays: blocking punts, intercepting passes, and sacking quarterbacks with such regularity that he set the all time sack record at Georgia. It was fitting that on his last play as a Georgia Bulldog he would end his career with a big play almost identical to the one at South Carolina. It came at a critical time!

It was January 1, 2005 in the Outback Bowl in Tampa, Florida with Georgia clinging to a shaky three point lead and Wisconsin driving deep in Georgia territory with about six minutes remaining. Wisconsin had the momentum and Pollack came up with one last great gem of a play. He avoided two blockers and sacked the quarterback, stripping him of the ball. It was almost identical

to the South Carolina play without scoring a touchdown. Pollack ran off the field for the last time as a Bulldog to watch the offense run out the clock. The game ended with the Bulldog's victorious, 24-21. Pollack had saved another game.

Every member of the Bulldog nation shed a tear when Pollack left the field for the last time, but nobody more than his position coach, Jon Fabris. More than anyone else, Fab knew what a crown jewel that he had in his defensive end. He loved him as a player and he loved him as a person. He summed Pollock to a "T" calling him a "fun loving caustic needler. A character with character."

Pollack could describe his coach the same way. Fab, as he is popularly called, is a "character with character" himself. I have admired him for many reasons especially for his sense and appreciation of history. In paying the ultimate tribute to his superstar, Fabris took a quote from his favorite movie and one of mine, "Chariots of Fire."

He recalls the scene in the true story about the 1924 Olympics when rising track star Eric Liddell was running the 440-meter in a dual meet between Scotland and France. At the meet to observe Liddell was Sam Mussabini, the internationally known and respected track coach. Shortly after the race started, Liddell apparently was bumped and rolled off the track. To the amazement of all, but perhaps not Mussabini, Liddell got up and started running again. Miraculously, he won, broke the tape and fell, completely exhausted. Liddell's young friend and trainer ran over quickly to embrace and help him. Mussabini came up to the young trainer and told him, "You better take good care of this lad as you will never find another like him."

DAVID GREENE
TO
MICHAEL JOHNSON
VERSUS
AUBURN UNIVERSITY
NOVEMBER 16, 2002

"Georgia had been behind all night. Greene's 'Hail Mary' pass to Johnson saved the day and set the stage for the SEC championship."

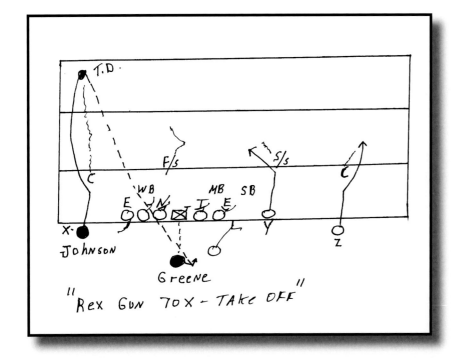

Georgia's quest for the first SEC Eastern Divisional title under mark Richt looked bleak at Auburn with the seventh ranked Bulldogs down, 21-17. It was fourth and fifteen on the Auburn 19-yard line with only 1:31 minutes left on the clock.

I was in the visiting athletic director's booth at the time thinking that it was all over unless some miracle takes place. Coach Mark Richt has often been accused of having a "hot line to heaven" and I became a believer after I saw the sensational finish.

Georgia had been behind all night. After the first half Auburn led, 14-3. It could have been worse. The Bulldogs battled back in the second half to get within striking distance after cutting the lead to 21-17 with a long touchdown drive in the third quarter. The scored remained unchanged when the Dawgs gained possession of the ball at their 41 yard line for the last time late in the fourth quarter. David Greene found Fred Gibson for a 41-yard gain to move the ball to the Auburn 14-yard line. Three incomplete passes exacerbated by a five yard false-start penalty brought up a gloomy fourth down with fifteen yards to go at the 19 yard-line. The ball was on the left hash mark. Coach Richt called for "Rex Gun 70 X Take Off." "Rex Gun" was the formation, "70" the protection, and "X-Take Off" was a deep fade route.

Greene said, "I was a little surprised at the call, since it was a play that had not really been called that season. It was a play that we didn't normally work on, but we had reviewed it once or twice." It is amazing that Greene remembered the play and I recall Coach Richt complementing 'Greenie' on his recall and execution.

The play called for Greene to pump fake downfield to the wide side and throw a take-off deep pass to the left split-receiver, Michael Johnson. Offensive coordinator and quarterback coach Mike Bobo said that the play "was basically a Hail Mary to one receiver." The pump fake was important since the tight end blocked, which could have caused their free safety to doubled cover Johnson. Bobo remembered that, "When Greene pumped to the field, the free safety set his feet." Greene reset and threw it to the back pylon to Johnson who was behind the corner. Johnson, with a slight body nudge, went up and over the smaller Auburn cornerback catching the ball at "its highest point" to make the score 24-21.

Johnson was the ideal receiver for the "one man Hail Mary" pass. He was 6'3" and 230 pounds, very strong, and had been an excellent high school basketball player. "I knew Michael would go get it," said Greene. Coach Richt said, "I felt like if anybody would win a jump ball, it would be Michael. Fred Gibson, with his injured thumb in a cast, would have trouble reaching up with two hands." Johnson had little trouble leaping up with two hands over Auburn's cornerback. "I wasn't even open," Johnson said, "but I had to make the play." Johnson had a game of a lifetime substituting for the injured Terrence Edwards, the SEC's eventual all-time leader in receiving yards. Johnson caught thirteen passes for 141 yards, including the sensational, leaping basketball style catch for the winning touchdown and SEC title opportunity.

The improbable catch put Georgia in the SEC championship game. The Bulldogs soundly whipped the Arkansas Razorbacks winning the first conference championship in twenty years.

Greene's touchdown pass to Johnson in 2002 immediately drew comparisons from the old grads of Fran Tarkenton's touchdown pass to Bill Herron forty-one years earlier in 1959. Both touchdowns came in the closing seconds of the games on fourth down against Auburn though at different locations. Both plays were responsible, either directly or indirectly for winning the SEC championship. And both plays became among the most memorable in Georgia's football history.

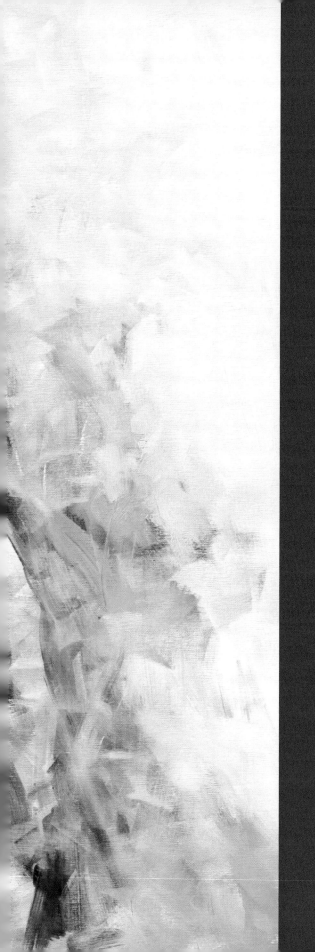

MATTHEW STAFFORD
TO
MIKEY HENDERSON
VERSUS
UNIVERSITY OF ALABAMA

SEPTEMBER 22, 2007

One of the key football games for Coach Mark Richt's Georgia Bulldogs early in that comeback and magical 2007 season was against Alabama in Tuscaloosa. Spirits were high at the "Capstone" under new Coach Nick Saben, especially after the Crimson Tide had beaten highly ranked Arkansas in overtime. That victory had vaulted them to a No. 16 ranking. Georgia was coming off a very disappointing conference loss at home to South Carolina. The defeat almost dropping them out of the top twenty-five nationally. The game was a sellout with over 92,000 fans in Bryant-Denny stadium that night. Millions more watched on national television.

Georgia led in the fourth quarter, 20-10, but the Crimson Tide stormed back tying the game, 20-20, and sending it into overtime. Alabama scored first with a field goal to make it 23-20. The Bulldogs needed a touchdown to win. Georgia got it on a first down play that surprised everyone in the stadium and stunned the Alabama fans. On Georgia's initial play in overtime, Offensive Coordinator Mike Bobo, who was calling plays for the first time, called "R-Yo to L, 142 Z-take-off." "R" meant formation right, "Yo to L" meant tight end motions left, "42" meant play action, fake isolation to tail-back, and "Z-take-off" is a deep corner route.

Bobo felt that since they had been running the isolation or fullback lead play all night out of the Y motion set, that it was a good opportunity for the defense that Alabama had been consistently lined up in on first down. Bobo knew that Alabama favored a single safety with corner back press coverage to the outside. When Bobo saw the alignment, he knew that speedy Mickey Henderson – nicknamed "Blur" by his high school coach -- had a good chance to beat the corner back off the line of scrimmage. The play fake by the quarterback Matthew Stafford to the tailback held the safety, keeping him from covering Henderson deep. The offensive line was in maximum slide protection. After Stafford pump faked to the right, laid the ball in the left corner where Mikey made a great catch over the shoulder! The twenty-five yard pass completely sealed the victory over the Tide, 26-23.

Bobo's rationale for the call made great sense. He did not want Alabama to become excited if the Crimson Tide stuffed a run on first down. He further felt that the pass percentage was safe. Moreover, since Alabama had scored in overtime, he "felt that the kicker could make a field goal to tie if Georgia failed to score a touch-down." With the predictable coverage by Alabama on first down

"Alabama was a critical game in Georgia's magical comeback season in 2007, and this play in overtime became one of the most memorable plays the Richt era."

Bobo felt it was the best chance "to win the game right there."

Henderson told me that he was so focused when his number was called that after the catch he didn't understand "why everybody was running on the field celebrating." He started shouting not comprehending the game was over, "We got to kick the extra point!" About that time Chester Adams, a 330 pound offensive lineman named "Cheese" was the first teammate to reach Henderson and hugged him with an old pro wrestling move described by corner back Thomas Flowers as a "Frog Splash." The rest of the team followed Adams and piled on Henderson. "I felt like the pile was six feet high," Henderson said. "I heard Cheese say that he couldn't breathe. When I heard Cheese say that, I knew that I must have been in trouble, too."

While there were other challenges during the season, the Bulldogs ended up ranked No. 2 in the nation after a convincing win in the Sugar Bowl! Arguably the Bulldogs could have been the best team in college football at the end. This would never have happened without the Stafford to Henderson play in overtime in Tuscaloosa. That play will go down as one of the most memorable play in the Georgia-Alabama series and also one of the most memorable in Georgia's football history.

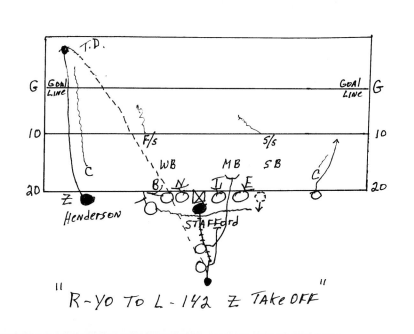

"R-YO TO L-142 Z TAKE OFF"

The Kickers

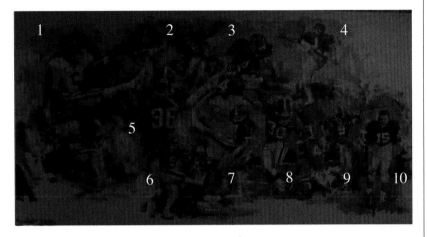

I have chosen my final of the thirty-four plays featured in this book as a group. I must pay tribute to many of the great Bulldog kickers. Of course, Hall of Famer Kevin Butler's 1984 kick was singled out, and set the bar for memorable, last-second field goal victories. However, since 1960 there have been nine other Bulldog kicking heroes who performed similar victory feats. Together, to my thinking, they comprise the thirty-fourth and final "most memorable" play (or set of plays) in Georgia football history.

Kevin Butler (1) (featured earlier in the book)

Durwood Pennington vs. Mississippi State University
October 15, 1960 (10)

Pennington was labeled the "automatic toe" by Georgia publicist Dan Magill for his kicking dependability. He was no stranger to clutch kicks. In the Auburn game in 1959 he kicked the extra point with thirty seconds left to give Georgia the win, 14-13, and the SEC championship. In the Mississippi State game in 1960, Pennington booted his last second field goal winner. He tied the game 17-17 with a field goal with six minutes left in the game. After the ensuing kick-off, Mississippi State had a long drive but missed a field goal with 3:39 to play.

Taking over on Georgia's own 20-yard line, Fran Tarkenton led the Bulldogs sixty-seven yards in seven plays to the Mississippi State's 13-yard line. With eight seconds left on the clock and in the game, Pennington made history by kicking the field goal to beat Georgia's "Bulldog Cousins", 20-17.

Kim Braswell vs. University of Florida
November 11, 1973 (4)

Braswell was a fiery competitor out of Avondale who wanted to complete other than just kicking. He was too valuable as a kicker to risk his diminutive body getting hurt so we converted him to a kicking specialist. Braswell was a left footed straight toe kicker that wore a hearing aid. He told me that when he was kicking that he always turned his hearing aid off to better concentrate. He obviously turned it off in the Florida game when he kicked the field goal with fifty seconds left on the clock to beat the Gators.

We were in a battle royal with Florida in the 1973 game which was usually always the case with this heated rivalry. We were down, 0-7, early in the fourth quarter when Buzzy Rosenburg intercepted a Gator pass. Two plays later Andy Johnson hit Rex Putnall for a 47-yard touchdown and we were tied, 7-7.

Late in the fourth quarter Dan Spivey caused a fumble that was recovered by Joe McPipken at the Florida 30-yard line. After a couple of running plays and with fifty seconds left on the clock, Braswell, 'trotted on the field' and kicked a 37-yard field goal to give the Bulldog Nation a thrilling win over the Gators.

Alan Levitt vs. Georgia Tech
November 27, 1976 (9)
Alan Levitt, from Brooksville, Florida, was the first pure field goal soccer kicker that we recruited. Levitt started a string of three consecutive All American kickers. He was our kicker for four years establishing several Georgia and SEC records.

In 1976, Levitt's senior year, we beat Florida and Auburn to win the SEC Championship. The Georgia Tech game was looked upon as somewhat anti-climatic which got us into trouble. After we went ahead, 10-0, Tech battled back in the fourth quarter with a touchdown and a field goal to tie the game at 10-10. With a little over six minutes in the game the Bulldogs responded like champions with our quarterback Ray Goff leading the team on a drive from our own 33-yard line to Tech's 31-yard line. However we lost the ball to Tech on a fumble, with 3:09 left on the clock. After a lot of 'moans and groans' Tech fumbled it back to us. We then drove to Tech's 15-yard line, taking off three minutes from the clock and with five seconds left in the game we called a time out sending Levitt in the game to kick the winning field goal.

I remember that the game was played in a bad fog that got progressively worse as the game went on. When Levitt went into the game to kick the fog had dropped so low that it covered the upper deck of the stadium. Lev-

itt's kick split the up rights and partially disappeared in the fog. We won, 13-10. It was Levitt's last play as a Bulldog 'between the hedges,' a memory for a life time.

Rex Robinson vs. University of Kentucky
October 28, 1978
All American Rex Robinson that 'kid out of Marietta,' as Larry Munson called him, was our kicker for four consecutive years. He holds several Georgia and SEC records and his 101 consecutive PAT's (points after touchdowns) is the second best in NCAA history.

For all of his accomplishments, Robinson is most remembered for his last second "wonder dog" field goal that beat Kentucky in Lexington in 1978. Kentucky completely out played us for three quarters. We were down, 16-0, but rallied late to close the gap to 16-7 going into the fourth quarter. We scored again with ten minutes left in the game to make it 16-14. Kentucky had a long six minute drive but missed a field goal and we got the ball back with 4:03 left to play. In a classic clutch drive led by quarterback Jeff Pyburn and tailback Willy McClendon, we drove 63-yard in ten plays and called time out on the 12-yard line with five seconds left. We sent in Robinson to kick the field goal, but Kentucky's coach Fran Curci, in an attempt to "ice" Rex called a time out. The time out was a blessing for us because we were short a lineman. Our tackle, Tim Morrison was on the sidelines praying and I told him that Coach Curci had answered his prayers. Robinson then kicked the winning field goal (29 yards) with three seconds left. Rex said "the whole field was pandemonium." During the kick Munson made his famous call, 'yeah, yeah, yeah'!

John Kasay vs. University of Arkansas at the Liberty Bowl

December 29, 1987 (7)

John Kasay was one of several second generation players that I had the privilege of coaching. His father, John Kasay, was an offensive guard on our 1966 SEC championship team. Big John Kasay was smart enough to direct his son to start kicking the football at a young age as opposed to grinding in the trenches as he had done. It was a very wise decision. John was one of the great kickers in Georgia's history but became the longest career kicker ever in the NFL by a Georgia Bulldog. As I reminisce about young John Kasay, I think of the name that Coach Erk Russell gave him when he was a little boy hanging around the locker room. Erk called him "Brief Kasay." While the subject is Kasay's field goal with 0:00 left in the game to beat Arkansas in the Liberty Bowl. I would be remiss not to mention another heroic Kasey kick. In 1996 Kasay kicked a 40-yarder with 1:31 left to beat Alabama between the hedges, 17-16. While the kick came with more than a minute to play, it sure qualifies as a memorable big play.

The Arkansas Razerbacks had dominated play most of the game and were leading, 17-7, going into the fourth quarter. Kasay closed the gap early in the fourth quarter with a 24-yard field goal to make it 10-17. After Kasay's kick off, we got the ball back after an interception by Jeff Beasley. Later quarterback James Jackson scored from the 5-yard line to tie the game, 17-17.

After battling back and forth in the closing minutes of the game, cornerback Carver Russaw intercepted an Arkansas pass and ran it back to the Razorbacks 43-yard line with only forty-six seconds left to play. Four plays later, including a key 16-yard pass to Troy Sadowski, we had the ball at the Arkansas 23-yard line and called time-out with :05 left on the clock.

I remember sending freshman, John Kasay, in the game and this left footed soccer kicker booted the ball that sailed in an unorthodox flight through the uprights! At that moment I flashed back in my mind to his daddy who played and worked for me and "little boy brief Kasay" hanging around the locker room and I felt like a proud granddad.

Kanon Parkman vs. Georgia Tech

November 23, 1995 (2)

Kanon Parkman was a solid field goal kicker for Georgia from 1991 through 1995. In 1992 he was redshirted while battling mononucleosis. It was in 1995 against Georgia Tech in Atlanta that he will long be remembered. He kicked a 34-yard field goal with :47 left on the clock to give the Bulldogs a memorable come-back victory against Georgia Tech.

It was Coach Ray Goff's last regular season game as Georgia's coach. Georgia was down, 17-7, to Tech at the start of the fourth quarter. Georgia closed the gap to 17-15 with a touchdown mid-way through the quarter. With 7:23 left in the game, Georgia drove 75-yards in sixteen plays from its own 10-yard line to Tech's sixteen. On fourth down and one, with :52 left Georgia called a time out and Parkman delivered a "line drive" darting kick that sailed through the uprights with :47 left giving Georgia the victory and a fitting farewell to Coach Ray Goff. This was Goff's fifth straight win over our state rivals at Georgia Tech. (6)

Hap Hines vs. Purdue University at the Outback Bowl
January 1, 2000 (3)

Hap Hines another "Kid out of Marietta" was a solid kicker for the Bulldogs from 1996-1999. He set two career bests in his last year with three field goals versus LSU (31,20,33) and four field goals against Ole Miss (27,23,51,48) which tied the school record. The last one, 48 yards, in the final minutes and gave Georgia the victory.

I will always remember Hap for his humanity and compassion toward a fellow kicker. Coach Jim Donnan's Georgia Bulldogs played Virginia in the Peach Bowl in a high scoring game. It was a game that appeared to be decided by who had the ball last. Georgia had the lead, 35-33, with Virginia driving in the final seconds to set up a relatively easy field goal that would give Virginia the win, 36-35. The Virginia kicker missed the chip shot and went to his knees in depression on the field. As Georgia celebrated, the Virginia team walked to the locker room disgusted completely ignoring their depressed teammate who was on his knees with his head bowed. Only Hap Hines, a fellow kicker, who actually knew the pain, came up and put his hands on the kicker's shoulder extending his consolation. That simple gesture did not go unnoticed and won for him (Hap) a National Sportsmanship Award. For all of Hap's accomplishments he will best be remembered for his 21-yard field goal in overtime that beat Purdue, 28-25, in the Outback Bowl in Tampa. Donnan's team staged the greatest come-back in bowl history, rallying from a 25-0 deficit with twenty-eight unanswered points to defeat the Boilermakers, 28-25. With minutes left in the game, Randy McMichaels caught Quincey Carter's an eight yard touchdown pass to tie the game, 25-25, and send the contest into overtime.

Georgia stopped Purdue on their first drive and their kicker missed a 43-yard field goal attempt. Georgia drove to the 11-yard line on its possession and Hines delivered a 21-yard field goal to complete the historical comeback.

Billy Bennett vs. University of Alabama
October 5, 2002 (8)

Billy Bennett came to Georgia as a walk-on from Athens Academy in 2000. Four years later, he became the most productive kicker in Georgia's history. At the end of his senior season he held thirteen Georgia records, seven SEC records and nine NCAA records. While all of his records are too numerous to mention it is worth noting a select few. He scored the most career points at 409 which were a Georgia and a SEC record. He also established a Georgia record and tied a SEC record by kicking six field goals in one game against Georgia Tech in 2001. His nine NCAA records were also Georgia and SEC records.

While he was a kick producer extraordinaire, I said on many occasions that he was given too many opportunities. During most of his career, Georgia's offense was not very productive scoring touchdowns especially in the "red zone." This gave Bennett many opportunities to kick field goals. On the other hand, to Bennett's credit he seized every moment, as evidenced by reviewing his NCAA records. He holds the record for the most field goals in a season with thirty-one, the most field goals made in a career eighty-seven, and the most field goals attempted 110.

Billy was an interesting character. He was only about 5'8" and a fiery competitor. He was a music lover and would often be seen playing the guitar with many different bands around town. His most memorable play came in 2002 when his 32-yard field goal with thirty-eight seconds to play enabled the Bulldogs to beat Alabama in Tuscaloosa for the first time ever. With 3:45 minutes to play, Damien Gary returned a kick fifteen yards to the Alabama 34-yard line. Georgia drove to the Alabama 15-yard line in seven plays with Musa Smith doing most of the running. On fourth down Georgia called a time out. Bennett entered the game and kicked the field goal beating Alabama, 27-25, for a great victory and setting the stage for Coach Richt's first SEC championship, and Georgia's first in twenty years!

Brandon Coutu vs. Vanderbilt University
October 13, 2007 (5)
All SEC Brandon Coutu was the catalyst who started the 2007 Bulldogs on what may be the greatest turn around in Georgia football history. After losing the first SEC game to South Carolina in Athens, Georgia went to Knoxville and was soundly beaten by Tennessee, 35-14. Despite the fact that Tennessee played well Georgia's performance was nonetheless one of the poorest in recent years.

The next week in Nashville, Georgia's performance was not much better and the Bulldogs were down, 17-14, mid-way into the fourth quarter. With 6:12 minutes left in the fourth quarter, Georgia drove to the Vanderbilt 13-yard line and Coutu tied the score, 17-17.

Vanderbilt took the next possession and in six plays was on Georgia's 18-yard line in position to regain the lead and possibly win the game. At that moment even the most optimistic Georgia supporter would not have predicted that this Georgia team on the brink of disaster mid-way through the season would end up winning the Sugar Bowl, ranked No.2 in the nation in the final poll. Vanderbilt on third down and four, at the Georgia 18-yard line, ran a play that gained eight yards to the ten where Darryl Gamble caused a fumble and Daniel Ellerbe recovered at the Georgia seven yard line.

With 2:43 minutes left to play, Georgia started a drive from the seven and went seventy-three yards in nine plays calling time-out on Vanderbilt's 19-yard line with 0:03 on the clock. Coutu's field goal of thirty-seven yards with 0:00 left on the clock gave Georgia the victory, 20-17, triggering the greatest turnabout in Bulldog history.

OTHER GREAT MOMENTS IN BULLDOG FOOTBALL HISTORY

ost Bulldogs fans can agree on the top ten or fifteen most memorable plays in Georgia football history, but beyond that opinions will vary greatly. There are numerous sensational plays made by Georgia's outstanding players. It is worth-while and fun to review some of those outstanding plays that arguably could have made the "Top 34"!

Bob McWhorter

Had it not taken place almost 100 years ago, a great case could be made for one play by Bob McWhorter, Georgia's first All-American. In 1910, McWhorter was instrumental in breaking the five year drought against Georgia Tech. Tech was leading, 6-0, in the fourth quarter, but McWhorter scored twice on runs of twenty yards and one yard to give the Bulldogs the victory, 11-6. (Touchdowns were worth five points from 1898-1911.) After McWhorter scored the second touchdown, excited Bulldog fans swarmed the field, causing a prolonged delay of the game. Finally with two minutes left the officials called the game, due to darkness.

John Roy Smith

In 1913, South Carolina had a 15-6 lead over the Bulldogs in a game played in Augusta. The Bulldogs rallied to score two touchdowns to win, 18-15. John Roy Smith, who lettered only one year for the Bulldogs, caught a touchdown pass in the last minute of the game to give the Bulldogs the victory.

James "Buck" Cheeves

In 1920, Georgia and Alabama, both undefeated, were playing for the Southern Conference Championship in Atlanta's Ponce de Leon Park. The Bulldogs were leading, 14-0, going into the fourth quarter. The lead appeared safe since the defense had not given up a touchdown all year. However, Alabama scored fourteen points to tie the score and then recovered a Georgia fumble on the Bulldogs twenty yard line. Georgia rose up and stemmed the Tide, holding 'Bama to three yards in three plays. Alabama sent in their ace drop kicker, Talty O'Connar, who had beaten the Bulldogs the year before with two field goal, 6-0. On the snap, Georgia's guard, Puss Whelchel, broke through the Tide line and blocked the field goal attempt. Quarterback, James "Buck" Cheeves scooped it up and ran eighty-five yards for the winning touchdown. The Bulldogs won the game, 21-14, and the Southern Conference Championship.

George Morton to Jack Curran

In 1926, Georgia rallied from a 13-0 deficit against Georgia Tech to win, 14-13. The deciding touchdown came late in the fourth quarter when Captain George Morton, on a roll-out pass, hit Jack Curran, who made a "leaping catch" in the end zone. H.F. Johnson kicked the extra point to give the Bulldogs a great comeback victory.

Jack "The Ripper" Roberts

The following year, after Georgia's great victory over Yale in the 1929 Dedicatory Game of Sanford Stadium, the next game in the series was played in the Yale Bowl in New Haven, Connecticut. Highly favored Yale lead, 14-6, in the third quarter and appeared to be well on its way to avenging the upset of the year before. Mistake after mistake by Georgia stymied any comeback hopes. Late in the fourth quarter, "Catfish" Smith caught a long touchdown pass to pull within two points, 14-12. Then in the last minute, Georgia reached the Yale 6-yard line, where fullback Jack "The Ripper" Roberts plunged over the goal line for an 18-14 victory.

"Buster" Mott

In 1931, Norman "Buster" Mott returned the second half kickoff ninety-five yards to beat New York University, 7-6, in the "Big Apple." The play enhanced his reputation as a party boy. He was earlier cited by Robert Ripley's syndicated cartoon, "Believe It or Not," for scoring long touchdowns the first two times he carried the football. He would always announce himself whenever he crashed a party with "Believe it or not, it's Buster Mott!"

"Scrappy" Moore

One of the grand 'ol coaches was the legendary Scrappy Moore, who coached the Chattanooga Moccasins for thirty-eight years. I have great memories of attending coaching clinics to hear him lecture when I began coaching. He was always the "life of the party." Before he entered the coaching profession, "Scrappy" quarterbacked the 1924 Bulldogs. He drop-kicked a memorable field goal in the forth quarter to break a scoreless tie and give the Bulldogs a 3-0 upset victory over Vanderbilt. The feat was especially memorable since "Scrappy" had never drop-kicked before and the team had no such kicking formation.

Cy Grant

In 1933, Cy Grant, long time principal of Georgia's first technical school located in Clarksville, executed a spectacular play against Georgia Tech that provided him memories for a lifetime. He caught a short pass from Homer Key and sprinted 65 yards for a touchdown. Grant then kicked the extra point to give the Bulldogs a 7-6 victory over their arch rivals.

Bill Hartman-Quinton Lumpkin

Four years later, in 1937, Georgia and Georgia Tech were again engaged in a great defensive struggle that ended 6-6. However, two Georgia heroes were prominent in denying Tech an apparent victory. All-American and Hall of Famer Bill Hartman returned a second half kick off ninety-three yards for a touchdown. All-SEC center and later beloved Georgia assistant coach Quinton Lumpkin blocked Tech's extra point to preserve the tie.

George Poschner

The 1942 Georgia-Alabama game has long considered among the greatest college games ever played by the 'Ol Timers. Undefeated, Alabama led, 10-0, for fifty minutes until Georgia rallied to victory, 21-10. All-American end George Poschner caught two sensational touchdown passes from Frank Sinkwich, to give Georgia the victory. The winning touchdown came on a "circus catch." Poschner caught the ball between two defenders and "came down standing on his head."

Johny Rauch

During his four years quarterbacking the Bulldogs (1945-1948), Hall of Famer and All-American Johny Rauch has so many big games that it is difficult to pin-point a single game or play as the best of his most memorable. In the undefeated 1946 season opener against Clemson, Rauch threw three touchdown passes; two of which were to John Donaldson, who became a long time great friend and coach on my staff. Rauch also had a "hot hand" that year in the Auburn game, throwing three touchdown passes again, as well as running for a touchdown.

However after talking to John he said that his most memorable game was against Georgia Tech in 1946 between the hedges. The Bulldogs came into the game 9-0-0 and ranked third in the country. Georgia Tech lost their first game to Tennessee, 13-9, but had reeled off eight straight victories and was ranked number seven in the nation. Tech, lead by quarterback Frank Broyles, (Arkansas' great coach and athletic director) was optimistic and excited about playing the Bulldogs. The optimism and excitement was short lived as Georgia trounced Tech, 35-7, to remain undefeated. Charley Trippi rushed for two touchdowns including a sensational 65-yard run. Rauch threw two touchdown passes; one to Trippi who reciprocated by throwing a touchdown pass back to Rauch.

Rauch said that Trippi's great throwing ability was utilized in Coach Butts' newly adopted "T Formation" by the center snapping the ball directly to Trippi at the left-halfback position. Rauch would "stagger his left foot as he most often did on many running plays which enabled the center to direct snap to Trippi. Rauch said that on other occasions he would "go in motion" which provided for other opportunities for Trippi to throw to him. Rauch recalled catching at least a dozen passes during the 1946 season including "five for touchdowns."

While the Tech game was most memorable to Rauch, many think that Rauch's finest hour might have been in his performance against a heavily favored LSU team in 1947. He threw three touchdown passes in directing "one of the most exciting victories ever in Sanford Stadium."

Ken McCall

With Rauch still at the helm, Georgia won another SEC championship in 1948 after defeating Georgia Tech in a hard fought contest. The game was clinched when Ken McCall returned a Tech punt fifty-four yards for the final score in a 21-13 thriller. Guy Tiller of the *Atlanta Journal* described McCall's exciting run: "The slippery little Georgia safetyman stood still and let the Jackets come to him. Then he bolted to the south sidelines. Two of Tech's players crashed into each other and two key blocks sprung McCall free and he raced 54 yards to a touchdown."

Pat Dye

All-American linemen Pat Dye, who later coached Auburn to four SEC championships, left an indelible mark on Bulldogs history. In 1960 he blocked a Georgia Tech extra point to give Georgia a 7-6 victory.

Larry Rakestraw- Don Porterfield

The Georgia-Auburn series is unique in many ways. At the forefront of the uniqueness of this ancient rivalry is a lack of a "home field advantage." In fact, based on the record of these two teams, it often has been a distinct advantage to be on the road. Since the series left the neutral site of Columbus in 1959 and went home and home, Auburn's record in Athens is 17-8, while Georgia's record in Auburn is 13-9-2.

One of the many classic and memorable games that exemplified the "road field advantage" took place when Georgia visited Auburn in 1962. The Tigers were heavily favored to beat the Bulldogs who had won only two games going onto the ninth game of the season. Auburn led, 14-7, at halftime but Georgia scored twenty-three points in the second half mainly on the strong arm of senior Larry Rakestraw who two years earlier had set an NCAA record against Miami with 407 yards passing in a 31-14 victory in the Orange Bowl.

In the Auburn victory, Rakestraw hit halfback Don Porterfield for three touchdowns. The three touchdown receptions remains a (tied) school record.

The game went back and forth. Georgia led, 17-14, on a Bill McCullough 48-yard field goal but Auburn responded by driving to Georgia's 13-yard line. On the next play, defensive back Joe Burson intercepted Kent's pass and sprinted eighty-seven yards to put Georgia ahead to stay, 31-20.

Rakestraw was named *Sports Illustrated* "Back of the Week" after leading the Bulldogs to a great upset of the Tigers.

The game reminds me of another Georgia quarterback, Paul Gilbert, who also led his team to a stunning upset of the Tigers at Auburn in 1970. Earlier, Gilbert had earlier been named Back of the Week by *Sports Illustrated* after coming off the bench with Georgia down by twenty-one points, to lead the team to a victory against South Carolina, 52-34, after being behind by twenty-one points. In the Auburn game Gilbert was sensational in leading Georgia to a 31-17 upset of a highly favored Auburn team which was headed to the Sugar Bowl.

There have been many other Bulldog upset victories lead by Georgia quarterbacks in Auburn. The most recent being in 2006 when Matthew Stafford passed for 219 yards and one touchdown and rushed for eighty-nine yards and a touchdown to upset the fifth-ranked Tigers. History continues to repeat itself.

Preston Ridelhuber

In 1964, Preston Ridelhuber had one of the greatest runs I had ever seen "between the hedges." He weaved and swirled his way eighty-two yards, falling exhausted in the end zone. Unfortunately it did not count. The play was called back for holding. Another "Ridelhuber Special," that was not called back, occurred the following year against Michigan in Ann Arbor, in 1965. Ridelhuber was running a quarterback sweep to the left on the 29-yard line, contained by Michigan, he reversed his field, swung back to the forty going all the way to the right sidelines and down to the Michigan 6-yard line before being tackled. On the next play he hit Pat Hodgson for the touchdown to give us a fantastic upset victory 15-7 over "Mighty Michigan."

Billy Cloer

Another memorable play came to my mind, when I recalled Billy Cloer recovering an on-side kick against North Carolina in Chapel Hill. In a wild contest we beat the Tar Heels 47-35, scoring four unanswered touchdowns. In the fourth quarter the go ahead came after "Little" Billy's giant.

Bobby Etter and "The Cannon"

In 1966 we were 8-1 heading for a showdown against undefeated Georgia Tech between the hedges. A small cannon was brought up from Columbus, Georgia and was given to the cheerleaders, captained by Don Sims, now head of the Chamber of Commerce in Thomasville. The cannon was to the fired when we scored. Tech scored first and led, 7-0, until Kent Lawrence returned a punt seventy yards to make it 7-6. Bobby Etter came in for the extra point. As he approached the ball, the cannon went off prematurely, distracting Etter, who missed the extra point, Tech keeping the lead. However, we did eventually win the game, 23-14. The Columbus delegation buried the cannon the following Monday in concrete in Chattahoochee River. While standing on the banks of the river in Columbus they read a proclamation stating that "the cannon would never again cause the Bulldogs to potentially lose a game." Interestingly the ex-cheerleader Sims waited twenty-five years before he confessed to me one night in Albany that he was the one responsible for the cannon "misfire." We had a great laugh and a libation in celebration.

"Spike" Jones

The next year, in 1967 against Auburn, in Athens, our punter "Spike" Jones recorded an 87-yard kick that broke the thirty-year record of eighty-two yards, set by Bill Hartman. Coach Hartman often campaigned to put an asterisk by Spike's name since the wind was such a factor in breaking his thirty-year record.

Jake Scott

In 1968, All-American and 1975 Super Bowl MVP safety Jake Scott had a big play in most every game we played. That year, one of the biggest plays came against Tennessee in Knoxville when he returned a punt for an amazing 90-yard touchdown. It would no doubt have been one of the "thirty-four" most memorable plays had Tennessee not tied us on the last play of the game. Jake had other big plays that year including two interception returns for touchdowns against Kentucky in Lexington.

"Buzy" Rosenburg

The greatest day for any Georgia punt returner came against Oregon State in 1971. The "Super Frog," Lemon "Buzy" Rosenburg returned five kicks for 202 yards, which is still a Georgia record. Two of those returns were for touchdowns which is still an NCAA record.

Jimmy Poulas

Jimmy Poulas' last second "over the top" touchdown against Georgia Tech in 1971 is among the most memorable plays, but it doesn't do the "Greek Streak" justice in promoting his uncanny running ability. He had two terrific runs for touchdowns in two different bowl games. Against North Carolina in the 1971 Gator Bowl, he sprinted for twenty-five yards for the only touchdown in the game to beat the Tar Heels, 7-3. In the 1973 Peach Bowl against Maryland, Poulas took a screen pass and rambled sixty-five yards to beat the Terrapins, 17-16.

John Jennings

That same year, earlier in the schedule against Ole Miss in Jackson, Mississippi, offensive guard John Jennings had a play offensive lineman only ream of. Jennings, called "Pie Face" by his buddy and teammate, the one and only Bob Poss ("Little Possy"), will modestly share his scoring highlight with anyone who will listen. On the handoff to tailback Ricky Lake, Jennings came off of his block just as Lake fumbled. Lake was hit hard by an Ole Miss linebacker just beyond the line of scrimmage. The ball bounced up in the air and Jennings caught the ball in the air in a dead run and raced thirty-nine yards for a touchdown!

Glynn Harrison

In 1974, "Gliding Glynn" Harrison had a "run for the ages" against the Florida Gators. He went eighty-six yards swerving, weaving, limp-legging and breaking tackles, before crossing the goal line. Unfortunately, like Ridelhuber a decade earlier, the incredible run was called back! The runs by Ridelhuber and Harrison were two of the greatest I ever saw and certainly the two greatest that never counted. However, Harrison, like Ridelhuber, had a run almost as exciting a year later against Georgia Tech in 1975 at Grant Field. Harrison went seventy-eight yards in the second quarter that enabled Georgia to go up 28-0 at halftime. We eventually won the game, 42-26.

Matt Robinson

Quarterback Matt Robinson, who alternated with Ray Goff on our 1976 championship team, had one of his best games against Alabama that will be remembered for decades to come. Alabama, which dominated the league in the 1970s, came to Athens with another great team. Right before halftime in a hard fought contest, Robinson completed a pass to Steve Davis on Alabama's 3- yard line. With nine seconds left in the half Robinson scored on an option keep to put us up, 7-0. Robinson later iced the game with a touchdown pass to tight end Ulysses "Pay" Norris that made the score 21-0. After the game, a celebration erupted that lasted all night long, closing Milledge Avenue. It was perhaps the greatest football victory celebration that ever took place on campus and in 'ol Athenstown. Classes on campus were cancelled the next week in celebration.

Johnny Henderson

An even bigger game took place that year in Jacksonville against the Florida Gators. Ray Goff had his "day in the sun," accounting for five touchdowns. He ran for two and passed for three. However, it was no cake walk as Florida led, 26-13, at halftime. Momentum shifted in the second half as we staged a comeback. What really poured fuel on the fire was a great defensive play by cornerback Johnny Henderson, son of former Georgia football-baseball great, Billy Henderson, and one of the greatest high school coaches in the history of the state. Florida had the ball on its own 29-yard line, fourth and one. Florida Coach Doug Dickey decided to gamble and go for broke with an option pitch. Henderson threw the Florida back for a five yard loss, which set up a Bulldog touchdown. We went on to score four unanswered touchdowns winning, 41-27, en route to the SEC championship. The play was dubbed by the media as "Fourth and Dumb," and it will remain that way in the minds of many Bulldog fans.

Lindsay Scott

Lindsay Scott will always be known for his last minute catch and run in the Florida game to beat the Gators in 1980. However, knowledgeable Bulldog fans will never forget his 99-yard second half kick-off return against LSU in 1978 that propelled our team to a 24-17 victory against the Tigers in Baton Rouge.

Willie McClendon

That same year, 1978, tailback Willie McClendon ran for 149 yards against VMI (Virginia Military Institute) in Athens, breaking Frank Sinkwich's thirty-seven year season rushing record of 1,103 yards. Willie rushed for 1,312 yards which is still a school record for a senior. He only kept the season rushing record for two years until Herschel Walker broke it in 1980, establishing an NCAA season freshman rushing record of 1,616 yards.

Greg Bell- Freddie Gilbert

Some of the significant but less memorable plays in 1980 were mentioned when discussing the "Big 34" during that National Championship year. A very important play got us going in Auburn that year as the Tigers were giving us fits early on. Auburn was punting from mid-field and corner back Greg Bell blocked the kick. Defensive tackle Freddie Gilbert caught it on the bounce and 'long-legged' it twenty-seven yards for the momentum-changing touchdown.

Dale Carver - Stan Dooley

On Monday night at 9:00 P.M. in a Labor Day game in 1982 on national television in Athens, end Dale Carver blocked a punt against Clemson, the 1981 National Champions. Stan Dooley recovered the kick and fell in the end zone. The touchdown gave us an exciting 13-7 victory in a game that ended after midnight; leaving a bunch of happy but sleepy Dawgs at work on Tuesday the next day.

Tony Flack

In 1983 we were leading Georgia Tech, 27-24, but Tech was driving with about 1:30 left on the clock. Tech threw a pass that would put the Yellow Jackets in the position to win. Corner back Tony Flack made a game-saving interception with 1:22 minutes left to preserve another memorable victory over the Yellow Jackets, 27-24.

Charlie Dean

In the same year's season opener, on national television against UCLA in Athens, we were clinging to a 12-8 lead in the final minutes of the game. However, UCLA had a good drive going, penetrating inside our 49-yard line. Their quarterback, Rick Neuheisel, who returned as the Bruins' coach in 2007, threw a pass that was intercept-ed by Athens' native Charlie Dean. He raced sixty-five yards to score the touchdown that gave us a 19-8 victory with eleven seconds left. The game ended at 12:15 A.M. on September 4 (my birthday) and Charlie and the team presented me with the best birthday present I could ever remember!

John Lastinger — 99 yards

Before John Lastinger's "Glory, Glory" touchdown run against Texas in the Cotton Bowl after the 1983 season, he led a "Glory, Glory" drive against Florida that will never be forgotten. Trailing 9-3 in the fourth quarter, we found ourselves backed up on our own 1-yard line. Lastinger took the team, ninety-nine yards in sixteen plays to give us a 10-9 victory over the Gators. The score set the stage for the 10-9 victory in the Cotton Bowl where the time still remains in Dallas "10-9"!

Keith Henderson-Tim Worley

In recalling those great moments of the 80s, Georgia Fans will recall the 1985 Florida game when we faced the number one ranked Gators whose lofty ranking was short lived. Keith Henderson rushed for 145 yards with two touchdowns on runs of 76 and 32 yards. His running mate, Tim Worley, had 125 yards including an 89-yard run to clinch the victory, 24-3. The Gators managed only a field goal, thanks primarily to the play of Greg "Muddy" Waters who had thirteen tackles, two pass break-ups, caused an interception and had a sack against the Gators. The Bulldog faithful had one of its happiest days in Jacksonville, celebrating the victory over the Gators and their brief number one ranking!

Andy Dodson

While I was coaching, we gave stars on the head gear for extraordinary plays. Coach Richt changed the stars to "Dawg Bones". We also gave "Dawg Bones" but they were for game-saving feats only. Naturally, very few players ever got a "Bone" during the season. Our defensive tackle Andy Dodson earned a "Bone" for his play against South Carolina in 1986. We were in a "shoot out" with South Carolina that night in Columbia. We were up, 31-26, with 1:36 minutes left and could not stop the Gamecocks who were driving for the potential winning touchdown at out 11-yard line. Their quarterback, Todd Ellis, threw a pass to a wide open Sterling Sharp later of Green Bay Packers and NFL TV fame. The pass was a 12-yard curl and the ball bounced off his chest into the waiting arms of Dodson on our five-yard line. Andy had rushed the passer and when the ball was thrown, he turned and sprinted for the ball (we coached that fundamental but seldom successful execution) popped into his hands for a game-saving interception. We ran the clock out in three plays. Dodson became the proud recipient of a rare "Dawg Bone" on his head gear.

Steve Boswell

Linebacker Steve Boswell earned a "Dawg Bone" a few years later against Auburn. We were winning late in the game in 1986 against a heavily favored Auburn team in Jordan-Hare Stadium. Wayne Johnson, who filled in for James Jackson at quarterback, had a super night. We were up, 20-16, late in the fourth but Auburn was driving. The Tigers penetrated deep into our territory with a minute left to play. Boswell intercepted an Auburn pass with 58 seconds left to preserve the victory and earn himself a prestigious "Dawg Bone"! The excited Bulldog fans that stormed the field that night got an unexpected "shower" that they will never forget. Despite the hose job, all the Bulldogs were happy with the great upset victory over the Tigers.

Johnson- Hampton in the Gator Bowl

It is only natural that my last game as Georgia's coach is high among my fondest memories especially since we won. January 1, 1989 we beat a fine Michigan State team in the Gator Bowl, 34-2. It was a wide open game as both teams had over 400 yards of offense. Most of that yardage came in the air.

Since we traditionally had been a running team, most people were surprised we had taken the airways in my last game. It really should not have been so surprising since in our last regular season game against Georgia Tech we passed for a lot more yardage than we rushed in a 24-3 victory. In the Tech game we better utilized the throwing ability of quarterback Wayne Johnson. Johnson began throwing early against Michigan State. His primary target early on was our tailback Rodney Hampton one of the most versatile running backs I ever coached. Not only did Hampton have more different moves as a running back than any I had the privilege to coach, he was also an excellent receiver. He caught two passes for touchdowns in the first half giving us a 17-7 halftime lead over the Spartans.

Johnson continued his aerial assault in the second half hitting our tight end Kirk Warner for a touchdown. Steve Crumley kicked a field goal to make it 27-13. We were about to put the game away when super receiver Andre Rison, later of NFL fame, caught his second touchdown pass of the night, a 55-yard reception to make the score 27-20. Hampton responded this time on the ground rambling thirty-two yards for a touchdown to make it 34-20.

The lead once again looked safe but Rison caught another beauty for fifty yards to make the score 34-27 with almost 4:00 minutes left on the clock. By that time I had seen enough of Rison, and I didn't want him to have another opportunity to catch the ball.

So I ended my career like it started, by running the football. Hampton, who had a great pro career with the New York Giants, led the way as we ran nine straight plays on the ground to kill the clock. I had ended my coaching career in Jacksonville in the Gator Bowl in the same place I ended my playing career 34 years earlier. It was a most memorable night.

Garrison Hearst

A selfish thought came to me in 1988 while I was wrestling the decision to give up coaching the Bulldogs. I knew if I did, I would not have a chance to coach Garrison Hearst. I had scouted him in high school at Lincolnton and knew he was going to be an impact player. I made the right decision but have often thought how much fun it would have been to coach this All-American who won the Doak Walker Award given to the country's most outstanding running back.

Coach Ray Goff had the privilege to coach Hearst who helped Coach Goff to many victories. It was Hearst's magnificent 69-yard run on the toss sweep against Georgia Tech in 1991 that enabled the Bulldogs to win, 18-15. The victory broke Tech's two game winning streak and gave Coach Goff his first of five wins over the Yellow Jackets.

Hearst ended his career at Georgia with 3,232 rushing yards a school record second only to Herschel Walker. Lars Tate our great tailback from 1984-87 was another great rusher and ranks third in the Georgia record book for most career rushing yards. Herschel is of course in a class by himself by rushing for 5,259 career yards which is still a Georgia and SEC record.

The Clock Ran Out — On Auburn

In 1992, Coach Goff's team beat Auburn in Auburn in a memorable game. It was not a great or memorable play that made the game distinctive. What was most remembered was the clock running out and what happened just before the game ended. After Garrison Hearst scored his second touchdown to put Georgia up, 14-10, Auburn with no time-outs drove inside Georgia's one yard line. Auburn's ball carrier had run out of bounds, stopping the clock with nineteen seconds left. On the next play Auburn fumbled and there was a mad scramble for the ball that was eventually awarded to Auburn. The Tigers were frantically trying to line up to run another play, however, due to some Bulldogs who were intentionally slow getting off some Auburn players, and not to mention poor game management by the officials, the clock ran out. The Bulldogs won, 14-10, despite the protests of Auburn's coaches, players and fans.

Eric Zeier

By the time All-American Eric Zeier finished his career at Georgia in 1994, he became the most prolific quarterback ever to play for the Bulldogs. He set fifty-four school records and eighteen SEC marks. For all of the great games during his amazing career, the Florida game of 1992 was one of his best. Unfortunately, it ended as a sad memory. Zeier kept bringing the Bulldogs back answering scores of the high powered Florida offense. With Florida leading 33-26, Zeier led his team to Florida's 12-yard line with five seconds left. Zeier then hit Jerry Jerman on a slant route for the touchdown. The score could have tied or won the game based on the two-point decision; unfortunately the opportunity for a decision never happened as one official came running to the line of scrimmage indicating a Florida called 'time-out' before the snap. In fact television covering the game clearly showed that Zeier was back to pass before Florida's "Phantom time-out" was called. The fourth down was replayed and Georgia was unsuccessful, giving Florida the victory. Today's instant replays would never have allowed such a travesty of justice to take place.

Will Witherspoon

In 1999, Georgia linebacker and NFL great Will Witherspoon made one of the most athletic plays I ever saw in Sanford Stadium. LSU completed a 39-yard touchdown pass with eighteen seconds left on the clock to pull within one point of the Bulldogs, 23-22. On the two-point conversion, the LSU quarterback rolled right, stopped and threw back to a wide open Tiger receiver for the potential game winning two-point conversion. At the last second, Witherspoon "came out of nowhere" and with a Michael Jordan type leap knocked the ball down to preserve the victory.

Jamie Henderson- Corey Robinson—Interceptions

That same year, Jamie Henderson intercepted a Central Florida pass on the last play of the game to preserve yet another one point victory, 24-23. The following year in 2000, another interception preserved a victory for the Bulldogs in a wild scoring affair in Lexington. Corey Robinson intercepted a pass with 00:48 seconds left on the clock to preserve a 34-30 win.

Sean Jones

The most memorable and significant fumble recovery for a touchdown I ever saw took place in Knoxville, Tennessee, in 2003. Georgia was leading, 13-7, but Tennessee, on a long drive, reached the Bulldogs one-yard line in the final seconds of the half. On the next play, which more then likely would have given the Vols the lead, and the momentum at half time, Tennessee fumbled and Sean Jones picked up the ball on the eight and raced ninety-two yards for a touchdown with 00:07 left on the clock. It was a fourteen point turn-around that completely demoralized the Vols as Georgia went on to win, 41-14.

The Bailey Brothers and Reggie Brown

In 2002, Coach Mark Richt led Georgia to its first SEC championship in twenty years. In the Tennessee game that year, Georgia was locked up with the Vols in a mighty defensive struggle. As is usually the case in such a tight contest, the kicking game becomes a major factor. Boss Bailey, who holds the record for the highest vertical jump in Bulldog history, and Reggie Brown, who was second in the vertical leap, both played significant roles in Georgia's win; mainly through the kicking game. Brown blocked an early Tennessee punt that resulted in a safety and a 2-0 lead. Later Tennessee was attempting a field goal that would have put the Vols up 3-2; however, Bailey blocked the kick leaping higher then any Bulldog I can ever remember in a football game. Billy Bennett kicked two field goals, and Brown scored the only touchdown on a reception from David Green to give Georgia an 18-13 victory.

All-American Boss Bailey is the younger brother of Ronald and Champ, of the amazing Bailey Family. All the brothers played football at Georgia. Champ, an All-

American like his brother Boss, became the most versatile player in modern Bulldog history; playing offense, defense and on the special teams. He displayed his incredible athletic ability by setting the football vertical jump record in 1998 at 42 inches. The record stood for four years, until the summer of 2002 when Reggie Brown, in a morning workout, set a new record of an amazing 43 ½ inches. That afternoon "Boss" walked into the workout room and was greeted by Coach Dave Van Halanger, Georgia's ultra successful strength and conditioning coach. Van Halanger told Boss that "the Bailey legacy was done" announcing that Brown had jumped "off the chart" in breaking his brother's vertical leap record. Shortly thereafter, Boss, obviously challenged by Coach Van's words, jumped an incredible 46 inches to set a new Georgia record! Once again a Bailey was on top of the "Leaping Bulldog Leader Board"!

Odell Thurman

The longest and most memorable touchdown pass interception ever in Sanford Stadium took place by linebacker Odell Thurman in 2003. Georgia held a solid 19-0 lead going into the last quarter. Auburn, however, mounted a drive early in the fourth quarter going all the way to Georgia's two yard line. On third and two, Auburn's pass was tipped and Thurman picked it off and racing 99 yards scored, giving the Bulldogs a relatively easy 27-7 victory.

D.J. Shockley- Tim Jennings

In 2005 Georgia clinched its second SEC championship under Coach Mark Richt. Quarterback D.J. Shockley led the team to the SEC Eastern Division championship after beating Kentucky. However, the following week the state championship was very much in doubt in the annual battle against Georgia Tech that took place in Atlanta. Georgia was finally able to break a 7-7 tie when Shockley hit Bryan McClendon (son of former Bulldog running back and Coach, Willie McClendon) with a 19-yard touchdown pass with 3:18 left in the game. With plenty of time left on the clock, Georgia Tech mounted a drive that was finally stymied when cornerback Tim Jennings intercepted a Reggie Ball pass at the five-yard line with less then two minutes to play. The following Saturday, back in Atlanta for the SEC Championship game, Shockley threw two touchdown passes against LSU routing the Tigers, 34-14.

Joe Cox

In 2006 Coach Mark Richt faced one of his most challenging seasons. Losses to Vanderbilt and Kentucky sent the Bulldog nation into despair. It could have been worse had it not been for reserve quarterback Joe Cox. A very poor Colorado team had the Bulldogs on the ropes in the closing minutes, 13-0, between the hedges. Coach Richt inserted reliever Cox, who threw a touchdown pass to Brannan Southerland with 9:11 left to cut the Buffalo lead to 13-7. Cox then led the team down the field and with 00:46 seconds remaining hit Martrez Milner for a 20-yard touchdown pass giving Georgia the 14-13 victory over the Buffaloes following Brandon Coutu's extra point.

Tony Taylor

After the two conference losses to Vandy and Kentucky, the Bulldogs upset Auburn at Auburn. Georgia went on to defeat Georgia Tech and Virginia Tech in the Chick-fil-A Bowl to finish strong. However, the game against arch rival Georgia Tech was a real struggle which turned into a defensive battle just like the previous year. The key play in the 15-12 Bulldog victory was made by linebacker

Tony Taylor, son of Nate Taylor, starting linebacker on the 1980 National Championship team. Tech fumbled the ball and neither team could get a handle on it. Taylor was standing and bent over the pile and picked the ball up and raced twenty-nine yards for a touchdown.

Coach Mark Richt - Fire and Enthusiasm

In 2007, after two uninspired performances back to back against Tennessee and Vanderbilt, Georgia appeared to be in trouble facing sixth-ranked Florida in Jacksonville. Coach Mark Richt re-committed himself to generate more fire and enthusiasm within himself and the team in the future. He went so far as to uncharacteristically order a celebration following his team's first touchdown. Coach Richt indicated he was referring to the offensive team celebrating, however, the entire team ran on the field and into the end zone to celebrate Knowshon Mareno's touchdown. It cost the Bulldogs two fifteen-yard penalties which aided the Gators, who scored in two plays on their next possession.

The celebration strategy was not well received by the SEC office and Coach Richt graciously made a public apology of instructing his players to break a rule. No one will ever know for sure what effect such a strategy had on the team. What we do know is that the team caught fire in the Florida game and whipped the Gators soundly. The team spirit and enthusiasm continued throughout the rest of the season. The Bulldogs won the rest of their games and ended up being ranked number two in the nation at the end of the season.

Especially memorable was the "Black Out" in the Auburn game with the team wearing all black jerseys and most of the crowd in Sanford Stadium decked out in black. The energy generated by the "Black Out" no doubt had a lot to do with the victory over Auburn.

Every year, expectations remain as high as they have ever been. No doubt years to come will produce many more memorable plays that the Bulldog faithful will savor forever!

AFTERWORD

I was in my den sitting in my lamé smoking jacket when my wiry wife (often referred to as "101 pounds of grit, gristle and ingratitude") came in announcing that "Vick" Dooley was calling from Athens. Although a college graduate who can name the capitals of many states (most of them in the Deep South), she had no idea who Vince Dooley was. She placed the phone in my trembling hands and changed the TV channel to "Cops".

The caller was indeed Vince Dooley, the University of Georgia's legendary Coach and Athletic Director who retired having won 201 games in over twenty-five seasons, including a national championship. Vince was his usual calm state while I was flopping around like a loose mullet in the bottom of the boat.

"Bob", he intoned, "Steve Penley and I are working together on a book presenting the UGA football team's finest moments and we would like to have you do an af-terward. Billy Payne will be writing the introduction and Penley thinks we can come up with something worthwhile and make a few quid in the process." I stammered, "Coach I would be honored to the brink of incontinence to work with you on all this and will give you some pages before the end of the week."

When my head began to clear and I took on a more reflective stance, it occurred to me that there was no reason these towering figures at UGA should invite a graduate of Mercer University to participate. I recall too the battles that Lewis Grizzard and I took part in when we were both writing alleged humor columns for the Atlanta Journal Constitution. He said Mercer was more convent than college and I replied by saying that Mercer obtained its charter in 1833 as a place for students who were too poor to go to Emory and too proud to go to the University of Georgia.

This, of course, was before UGA had a well deserved reputation for scholarship and one had to bring more to the table than an appetite to gain admission. In fact, I did send two daughters, Nona Begonia and, appropriately, Georgia, to UGA to gain sophistication and knowledge, and (this is true) both girls went on to take roller skating for credit. This was in the days when the top academic award in the UGA freshman class was the coveted "I can dress myself badge." How things have changed.

Another comment offered by Grizzard to my writing skills can be found on the jacket of a book which states "Bob Steed has done for the literary world what Jimmy Swaggert has done for cheap motels."

I came back with a blistering riposte to the effect that I knew that Lewis was not writing all of his columns as many of them had both a noun and a verb. As much as the folks at Georgia Tech hate to admit it "Go Dawgs" is a complete sentence.

Well, enough about the Mercer-UGA rivalry. In fact, that is far too much of the controversy. I still remained flummoxed about the decision to add me to this welcome enterprise created by Vince Dooley and Steve Penley, but my credo has always been "never look a gift horse in the mouth" (or any other orifice for that matter) and I decided this was a happy train and now was the time to jump on it.

There was a trace of logic in the line up. I had, in fact, discovered Penley living in a refrigerator carton in 1990. He was raised in Athens, Georgia and Macon, Georgia and attended undergraduate school at the University of Georgia. In between starts at UGA, Steve studied painting at the School of Visual Arts in Manhattan. He has lived in this neck of the woods—Atlanta and Carrollton—since 1990 with his wife and three children. My wife, also an artist, was Steve's first portrait commission outside of school exhibitions.

It was April 1992 when I first saw some of his outrageously energetic efforts in a midtown Atlanta restaurant. I was stunned by his energy, style and artistic abandon. I learned that he was the night bartender in the restaurant and so I sought him out on the telephone and commissioned the aforementioned painting of my wife. By December 1992 we couldn't get Steve off the telephone and it seemed that Atlanta couldn't get enough of his paintings. He and my wife mounted a joint exhibition in the winter of 1993 at the art-friendly Hastings Seed Company Gallery. Over 600 people came on a bitter cold night to see this enterprise (later dubbed "Art on Ice"), but it certainly can't be said that they gave the show a chilly reception. Instead, it proved to be an important launching pad for Steve's artistic endeavors and his fame spread in the ranks of Atlanta's art enthusiasts with the speed of a mail bag leaving a rail siding. He virtually painted his way through my law firm, King & Spalding, turning out commission after commission. At the same time I introduced him to my friend, the late Lurton Massey at Kilpatrick & Cody, with the same happy result.

It is a fact that Penley's timing has been impeccable as well. After years of art that virtually anyone could make - abstract expressionism, conceptual art, minimalism or "art" compositions made of florescent commercial grade light bulbs, there has been a triumphant return to the figure and Steve's work exemplifies and exploits his return with gusto. His work is large, colorful, engaging and energetic and is filled with American icons - political figures, movie stars, prize fighters, simple flowers, landscapes and more. He seems to reinvent himself at every turn, most recently with these heroic and colorful and strong scenes from the University of Georgia's golden gridiron days.

Vince Dooley and Billy Payne need no praise from this pudgy pundit to participate in this endeavor. As for Dooley, his record speaks for itself: 201 games over twenty-five seasons, including a national championship. Billy Payne, who brought the Olympics to Atlanta is the epitome of self-confidence. It was once said that it was refreshing to see how much confidence Billy has in himself, particularly in these troubled times when so many people believe in no God at all.

I commend this valuable history and all three of these University of Georgia legends to you without reservation. As for me, I am quite content to be tagging along.

Robert L. Steed
Atlanta, July 2008

References

Books

Asher, Gene. *Legends*. Macon: Mercer University Press. 2005

Barnhart, Tony. *What it Means to Be a Bulldog*. Chicago: Triumph Books. 2004

Cromartie, Bill. *Clean Old Fashioned Hate*. Gridiron Publishers. 2007

Dooley, Vince with Barnhart, Tony. *Dooley: My 40 Years at Georgia*. Chicago: Triumph Books. 2005

Dooley, Vince. *Developing a Superior Football Control Attack*. New York: Parker Publishing Company. 1968

Dooley, Vince with Giles, Blake. *Tales from the 1980 Georgia Bulldogs*. Sports Publishing LLC. 2005

Dooley, Vince with Smith, Loran. *Dooley's Dawgs*. Atlanta: Longstreet Press

Dooley, Vince. *Unpublished Records of Georgia Football*. 1964-1988

Dooley, Vince. *Unpublished Records of Georgia Football Playbooks*. 1964-1988

Garbin, Patrick. *Then Vince Said to Herschel...The Best Georgia Bulldog Story Ever Told*. Chicago: Triumph Books, 2007

Hix, Tim. *Georgia Bulldogs- Great Moments in Team History*. Morris Book Publishing: LLC, 2006

Magill, Dan. *Dan Magill's Bull-Doggeral*. Atlanta: Longstreet Press Inc. 1993

Outlar, Jesse. *Between the Hedges- A Story of Georgia Football*. Huntsville: The Strode Publishers. 1973

Samelson, Ken. *Echoes of Georgia Football*. Chicago: Triumph Books. 2006

Smith, Loran. *Beloved Dawgs*. Longstreet Press Inc. 2005

Smith, Loran. *Between the Hedges*. Longstreet Press. 1992

Smith, Loran. *Between the Hedges- 100 Years of Georgia Football*. Atlanta: Longstreet Press. 1992

Smith, Loran, with Grazzard, Lewis. *Glory Glory*. Atlanta: Peachtree Publishers Limited. 1981

Smith, Loran. *University of Georgia Football Vault*. Whitman Publishing LLC. 2007

Smith, Loran. *Wally's Boys*. Athens: Longstreet Press Inc. 2005

Stegeman, John F., and Willingham, Robert M. Jr. *Touchdown-A Pictorial History of the Georgia Bulldogs*.
    Athens: Agee Publishers Inc. 1982

Stegeman, John L. *The Ghosts of Henry Field*. Athens: The University of Georgia Press. 1997

Tarkenton, Francis, A. *No Time for Losing*. Westwood, New Jersey: Fleming H. Revell Company 1967

Thilenius, Ed, and Koger, Jim. *No Ifs, No Ands, A lot of Butts: 21 Years of Georgia Football*.
    Atlanta: Foote & Davies, Inc., 1960

Troy, Jack. *Leading a Bulldog's Life*. Atlanta: Foote & Davies Inc. 1948

University of Georgia Football Media Guides—1964-2007

Videos, Tapes, DVDs

Aguar, David and Aguar, Richard. "100 Years of Georgia Football"

Aguar, David and Aguar, Richard. "25 Years of Georgia Football-The Vince"

Aguar, David and Aguar, Richard. "Herschel at Georgia."

Clayton, Jimmy. Great Moments in Georgia Football. "Dooley Era"

Engel, Mark S., Aguar, David and Aguar, Richard. "100 Years of Red and Black"

Graham, Stephen, Klemp, Marc. "Behind the Hedges." WXIA TV Channel 11

Pennel, Tim. "1966 Games and Highlights"

Pennel, Tim. "Georgia versus Yale 1929"

Shehane, James F. "Vince Dooley Show 1988 versus TCU." WSBTV Channel 2

Tereshinski, Joseph. "Georgia Highlights—1989-2006"

Personal Interviews

Arnold, Amp; Belue, Buck; Bobo, Mike; Britt, Charley; Brown, Fred; Butler, Kevin; Davis, Lamar ' Racehorse'; Donnan, Jim; Dukes, David; Etter, Bobby; Fabris, John; Felton, Claude; Goff, Ray; Greene, David; Haynes, Verron; Henderson, Mickey; Hoage, Terry; Johnson, Andy; Lastinger, John; Lawrence, Kent; Magill, Dan; McCarthy, Chris; Moore, Kirby; Patton, George; Pollack, David; Rauch, John; Richt, Mark; Robinson, Matt; Rosenburg, Buz; Sapp, Theron; Smith, Loran; Stanfill, Bill; Tardits, Richard; Tarkenton, Fran; Towns, Bobby; Trippi, Charley; Van Halanger, Dave; Walden, Bobby; Walker, Herschel; Whittenmore, Charley; and Woerner, Scott